ITH JOURNEY

MW01060456

Telephone No. _____ Fax_____

E-mail_____

Other _____

Profession of Faith

_____ _____
Date   Place
(Of becoming a Professing Member (Confirmation))

_____ _____
Officiating Pastor   Sponsor(s)

_____
Date , Name of Church, and Location of Reception as a Professing Member, if transferred from another Church

_____ _____
Sending Church   Receiving Pastor

_____
Sponsor(s)

Reason for Removal or Withdrawal from Professing Membership:

_____
_____
_____

Date: _____

Restoration of Professing Membership:

_____
_____

Date: _____

Date of funeral/memorial _____
Place of service _____

Current Chronological Number _____

Name _____

Address _____

Date of Birth _____

Place of Birth _____

Parents _____

Baptism

Date of Baptism   Sponsor(s)

Place of Baptism

Officiating Pastor

Date of Reception as a Baptized Member, if transferred from another Church

Sending Church   City and State

Previous Church Associations (Use back of sheet if you need more space)

Transfer to another church or annual conference*
*In cases when professing members become clergy members of the annual conference.

Date _____

Notes _____

Receiving church or annual conference:

Address _____

Date of death _____

Officiating pastor _____

CATCH A
NEW LIFE

Connect With a Church

CATCH A
NEW LIFE
Connect With a Church

DEBI WILLIAMS NIXON

Abingdon Press
Nashville

CATCH A NEW LIFE:
Connect With a Church

Copyright © 2009 by Abingdon Press

Requests for permission should be addressed to Abingdon Press, 201 Eighth Avenue South, P.O. Box 801, Nashville, TN 37202-0801, U.S.A.

Unless otherwise noted, Scripture quotations are from the Holy Bible, Today's New International Version ®. Copyright © 2001, 2005 International Bible Society. Used by permission of the International Bible Society.

Scripture quotations noted THE MESSAGE are from THE MESSAGE. Copyright © by Eugene H. Peterson, 1993, 1994, 1995, 1996, 2000, 2001, 2002. Used by permission of NavPress Publishing Group.

This book is printed on acid-free, recycled paper.

10 11 12 13 14 15 16 17 18 – 10 9 8 7 6 5 4 3

MANUFACTURED IN THE UNITED STATES OF AMERICA

Contents

Acknowledgments

Becoming a new member of a local church is an important decision. For me, being a member in the local church has been one of the most transformative experiences of my life. I want to acknowledge the impact the members at The United Methodist Church of the Resurrection in Leawood, Kansas, have had in shaping me. Through this church body, I have experienced love, grace, inspiring worship, challenging teaching, accountability, friendships, and a vision for what it means to catch a new life living for Christ.

I want to acknowledge deep appreciation for the incredible ministry team I serve with at Church of the Resurrection. Your passionate commitment using your gifts to help others on their journey to know, love, and serve God inspires me daily. Thank you, also, to Darrell and Dagney who served as writing contributors to this book.

I want to acknowledge my love and thanksgiving to my mom who made it a priority for us to be involved in church and Sunday school each week and to my dad who told me I could do anything. And finally, I want to express my deep love to Emily and Alex, my two amazing children, and Reed, my awesome husband. Your support and encouragement are a daily blessing. I love catching a new life with you.

Making the Commitment

Scripture Reading: Ephesians 5:25-30, (NIV)

Husbands, love your wives, just as Christ loved the church and gave himself up for her to make her holy, cleansing her by the washing with water through the word, and to present her to himself as a radiant church, without stain or wrinkle or any other blemish, but holy and blameless. In this same way, husbands ought to love their wives as their own bodies. He who loves his wife loves himself. After all, no one ever hated his own body, but he feeds and cares for it, just as Christ does the church—for we are members of his body.

Insight

One evening as Reed, a young college student, greeted me at the door of his fraternity house, there was an instant attraction and connection between the two of us. He immediately left his post and offered to show me around. In the months that followed, Reed and I began getting to know each other. We enjoyed jogging together, participating in college activities, studying together, and introducing each other to our families. I began to realize Reed might be the catch of a life, and he felt the same about me. So, we made a decision to make a deeper commitment. Reed asked me to be his bride, and I said yes to this lifelong commitment of loving and serving each other. As I write this chapter, this week marks twenty-five years of our marriage.

When Reed and I were married, we made a public declaration of our commitment to each other—a covenant saying, "I do," to love, serve, and be faithful to each other. The decision to become a member of a church is one by which people publicly declare their commitment to enter into a covenant with the church body, saying, "I do"—to love God and others and to be faithful to the church through attendance, spiritual growth, giving, and serving.

The church is described in the book of Ephesians as the bride of Christ. As

Jesus calls the church his bride, he invites us to the catch of a lifetime—to make a lifelong commitment to serving the church as a member of the body of Christ. But what is it that we are really making a commitment to?

We have come to misunderstand the church as a building, or the place where we go to attend a worship service, a funeral, or a wedding. But the biblical church is not a building or a place. The word *church* comes from the Greek word *ekklesia*, which is defined as "an assembly" or "called out ones." The root meaning of *church* is not that of a building, but of people.

Acts 2:42-47 gives us a glimpse of what it means to be the church. We see an assembly of people so overwhelmed by the love of Jesus they are gathered together to worship, study, pray, fellowship, and share meals. They also gave their resources to help others who were in need. This is the church in action faithfully entering into a committed relationship with Christ and one another. If you have become a member of a church, or if you are considering membership, you are saying, "I do," to be the church. You do not go "to" church. You are the church.

We respond to the call to be a member of a church as a tangible expression of the overwhelming love we have for Jesus Christ and the desire we have to be in relationship with him and with others. Through the church, you have the opportunity to experience the love of God in profound ways through a community of faith and to reach out to others with the love of Christ, helping to change the world. And through this experience, your life is changed, and you discover what it means to catch a new life.

Reflection Questions

1. What does the imagery of the church as the "bride of Christ" mean to you? *A public declaration and promise of dedication and commitment.*

2. What are your current thoughts about church membership? *Provides a community of people with similar faith and values.*

3. As you begin this look at what it means to be the church, write down any hopes, assumptions, and dreams you might have? *To help make a difference in my community (backpack buddies), provide a safe, healthy and spiritual environment for myself & my family.*

Action Step

Membership is an important decision, and as a member of the body of Christ you have a role to play. This handbook is designed to help you as you fully engage in the commitment you have made to be a member of the church. Over the next forty days you will have the opportunity to read a brief passage and complete a reflective activity or experience that focuses on the day's reading. Here are a few suggestions to help guide you in daily devotion each day.

1. Commit to a scheduled time to read and reflect each day. Set aside a minimum of 15 to 20 minutes.
2. Find a quiet place free from interruptions.
3. Begin in prayer, asking God to speak to you through the daily readings. You might pray a simple prayer such as *Dear God, I desire to know, love, and serve you more. As I study your word today, open my mind to discover more about the commitment I have made to be your church. Amen.*
4. Begin by reading the Scripture passage. You may want to read the verses preceding and immediately following the selected verses to get additional context and meaning. You can also read the Scripture in different translations using an online resource such as biblegateway.com or by using a variety of different Bibles such as the NIV or *THE MESSAGE*.
5. Read the brief insight, making notes or thoughts the writing brings to mind.
6. Respond to the questions, writing down your reactions. You will find your experience enriched if you take the time to write down your thoughts versus answering mentally in your head.
7. Each section ends with an action step. Making a commitment to do each of the action steps is an important part of the process.
8. Find a group of two to three others, and meet each week to discuss the weekly readings and to hold one another accountable..

Just as the vows spoken at a wedding bind a couple together in a covenant relationship, the vows you spoke or will speak when you join the church bind you in a covenant relationship with the body of Christ. Are you ready to discover what it means when you say, " I do"?

What Is the Church?:
The Old Testament Understanding of Church

Scripture Reading: Exodus 19:3-6

Then Moses went up to God, and the LORD *called to him from the mountain and said, "This is what you are to say to the house of Jacob and what you are to tell the people of Israel: 'You yourselves have seen what I did to Egypt, and how I carried you on eagles' wings and brought you to myself. Now if you obey me fully and keep my covenant, then out of all nations you will be my treasured possession. Although the whole earth is mine, you will be for me a kingdom of priests and a holy nation.' These are the words you are to speak to the Israelites."*

Insight

Self-starters, or entrepreneurs, are the ones who have begun just about every organization, business, sports team, charity, and school. An individual sees a need or an opportunity and finds a creative way to address it. When the idea works, it can change the lives of just a few families, a surrounding community, or potentially thousands of people for generations to come.

We owe a great deal to the vision and hard work of those who have passed on these legacies to us, which is why businesses and schools often bear the names of their founders.

Churches, too, are started by individuals or groups with a vision and a dream. Unlike other institutions and movements, however, human initiative and design did not result in the Church universal, the faith and the worshiping community that has existed for centuries. It was not the dream or the vision of any human being, nor did people invite God to join the work they were doing. Instead, God called people, and this calling dates back long before Jesus walked on earth.

The first book of the Bible, Genesis, is full of stories of individuals and families following God. Exodus, the book that follows and the book from which our scripture reading is taken, records God calling an entire people. God frees the Israelites from the bondage of slavery to Egypt, leads them through the wilderness to safety, feeds and cares for them, and then invites them into a special relationship. Through Moses, God tells them that if they are faithful to God, they will be a *"kingdom of priests and a holy nation."*

In the culture during the times of the Old Testament, priests of other religions served a unique function. They were the servants of the gods, responsible for appeasing the gods and bringing the sacrifices of the people to them. This role was a privilege but also a great responsibility, as the priests carried the weight of the people's relationship with the gods. If the gods became angry with the people, the priests must have failed in their duty.

By calling an entire nation as priest, the one true God was calling them all to serve God on behalf of the world. Unlike the other gods, who required sacrifice from people for their own voracious appetites, in God's kingdom, service to God is marked by service to the world, service to others. God requires justice and mercy (Micah 6:8), and these qualities are to be the identifying marks of God's people, God's priestly kingdom.

It is significant that God calls an entire nation of people collectively. We do not serve God's kingdom best as individuals, doing it on our own, but rather as a community. When the Israelites followed God's voice and remained faithful to their covenant relationship with God, they were a blessing to the surrounding nations and to the strangers in their midst. When, however, they stopped working together, followed their own selfish ambitions, or mistreated one another, not only did their community break down, they also did not fulfill what God had called them to do and to be.

These words spoken to the people of Israel in the wilderness are still spoken to the church today. We, as the church, are a priestly kingdom. This is a heavy responsibility, but also a great joy to live into. Although we will not always be perfect, we ask that God will continue to form us and to use us in ways that will bless the world.

Reflection Questions

1. In what ways does God's calling an *individual* look different from God's calling a people? *An individual is solitary in goal and purpose. A people provides a singular goal for many.*

2. How might the church be uniquely positioned to promote justice and mercy in your community? In the world?

3. Do you see yourself as part of a priesthood? What does this mean to you? *Yes, my participation in the community and world is a reflection of God in me.*

Action Step

As you think about the church as a kingdom of priests, contrast the difference between a church of only one individual and a church as a group of people. Look at the ministries of your church. What difference is your church making as a group of people that you could not do individually?

What Is the Church?:
Jesus Establishes the New Testament Church

Scripture Reading: Matthew 16:13-18

When Jesus came to the region of Caesarea Philippi, he asked his disciples, "Who do people say the Son of Man is?"

They replied, "Some say John the Baptist; others say Elijah; and still others, Jeremiah or one of the prophets."

"But what about you?" he asked. "Who do you say I am?"

Simon Peter answered, "You are the Messiah, the Son of the living God."

Jesus replied, "Blessed are you, Simon son of Jonah, for this was not revealed to you by flesh and blood, but by my Father in heaven. And I tell you that you are Peter, and on this rock I will build my church, and the gates of death will not overcome it.

Insight

Yesterday we looked at when God first called a people to be God's people. In today's scripture reading is the first time the word *church* appears in the Bible. Jesus is calling the church into existence from a group of people who, to everyone, including themselves, probably looked less than capable of establishing anything substantial. Yet they are brought together for a purpose. Jesus called them out.

The word *church* comes from the Greek word *ekklesia*, which means "a gathering of people who have been called out for a special purpose." Jesus is the first to apply this word to his disciples, who understood their role as a continuation of the calling of God's people in the Old Testament as a kingdom of priests. This description fits, but it is not the complete picture. The disciples are the beginning of a new movement, one that will invite people to join in a body that has a unique relationship to God through Jesus Christ.

When Jesus refers to the *church* he is not speaking of a building or a specific denomination, but rather to all people who follow him. He establishes his church with Peter and with the other disciples.

Jesus was, and continues to be, the builder; and so the church is dependent upon his power alone. Because the church is built by the power of Jesus, he can say confidently that it will withstand even the gates of Hades. In New Testament Roman times, Hades was believed to be the realm of the dead; so Jesus is declaring that even death cannot vanquish the church.

Whenever I hear stories of Christians around the world who gather for worship and study together while under the threat of violence or persecution for their beliefs, I am in awe. I wonder whether my faith would prove that strong and true, but I also marvel that the church not only survives but thrives in conditions created to squelch it.

In light of these verses, though, it should not be surprising, because in establishing the church Jesus promised that no power could overcome his power, that nothing would destroy his church. It is humbling to know that any success of the church is attributed to God's strength and not ours; it is also incredibly exciting to participate in something ultimately powerful and eternal.

Jesus continues to invite us to participate in the building of and being the church. Our purpose as the church is to make Christ known to the world. By becoming a member of the church, you are saying yes to being the church.

There is a difference between coming to church and being the church. When you are the church you take a different attitude. Instead of looking at the church as a place where you can have your needs met, you begin to look at church as a place where you can meet the needs of others—those for whom Christ died, those who are oppressed, those who hunger both physically and spiritually, those who are lonely and hurting.

As you consider this new life you are catching, what does it mean to be the church? What changes do you need to make so that Christ is the foundation of your spiritual life?

Reflection Questions

1. If someone were to ask you, "What is the church?" how would you answer? gathering of people

2. With Jesus as the builder, and the Spirit of God as its power, it may seem

as though the church could not go wrong. Unfortunately, this is not always the case. What might cause the church to become a destructive or powerless gathering of people?

When the people focus on their own wants and agendas instead of being prayerful and focusing on and listening to God.

3. When have you seen the church as a powerful force for God's purposes?

When helping others.   ie. Gift of Warmth Ministry "Identified a need and the need was served."

Action Step

We all carry with us a lifetime of experiences and perspective. On a blank sheet of paper, make two columns. In one column, write a list of negative adjectives that you have heard others use or perhaps that you yourself may have used to describe the church. In the other column, write a list of positive adjectives. Keep these lists in your Bible or another convenient place, and as you engage in the life of the church, consider how you can live into the positive side of the list you created.

Day 4

What Is the Church?:
The Church as the Body of Christ

Scripture Reading: Colossians 1:18-20

[Christ] is the head of the body, the church; he is the beginning and the firstborn from among the dead, so that in everything he might have the supremacy. For God was pleased to have all his fullness dwell in him, and through him to reconcile to himself all things, whether things on earth or things in heaven, by making peace through his blood, shed on the cross.

Insight

On Sunday morning, thousands of parents across the world wake up their children and help them prepare to "go to church." When there, the children learn all sorts of useful things, including the lesson that *church* is not a building or a place, but instead is the people. No wonder people are confused. How can children go to church when *church* is not a destination or a place? It is not surprising that even those who grow up in the Christian faith have a hard time naming what *church* is.

Faithful Christians have been developing definitions for *church* since New Testament times. For nearly two thousand years, theologians, clergy, and laity have been debating the issues of what defines the church, what the requirements are for membership, and what the church's mission should be. It would seem that, after 2000 years, we are no closer to a consensus than we were before. Ask 100 people to define *church*, and you will likely receive 100 different answers. Some will say it is a building, others will refer to a worship service, and others will call it a massive institution. Images and metaphors also abound. No one answer is the complete answer, but each idea and definition adds to our understanding of the essence and purpose of *church*.

18

The church as the body of Christ is perhaps one of the most well-known images of *church*. This is the language that the apostle Paul uses to describe the church in the scripture passage quoted above, and it is one of the most popular images throughout the New Testament. You will see this metaphor more in the days to come. To say that the church is the body of Christ is to imply at least two things about the nature of the church.

First, it names who is the ultimate authority of the church. If the church is the body of Christ, then Jesus is its head. Theologian Jürgen Moltmann put it this way: "It is only where Christ alone rules, and the church listens to his voice only, that the church arrives at its truth and becomes free and a liberating power in the world." (Moltmann, 5) The converse of this statement would be that when Christ does not rule, the church ceases to be the true church. This is a serious indictment against those who have tried to co-opt the church for their own purposes, starting with the first Christian Roman Emperor, Constantine, and including King Henry VIII, and Adolf Hitler. These are extreme examples that are easy to condemn, but churches in the United States in the 21st century are also vulnerable to giving up authority to one other than Christ.

The second implication of this image is the church's function. The body of Christ carries out Christ's mission that he began during his ministry on earth. Jesus summed up this mission in Luke 19:10: to "*seek out and to save the lost.*" This simple statement covers a broad ministry, as the lost covers all who suffer, from physical slavery to those in crisis to those who do not have an ultimate purpose in life. With this broad view of mission, it is easy to see how the whole body, not just preachers and pastors, must be involved in mission for the church to carry out its calling.

This image of the church as the body of Christ begins to help us see God's calling on our lives to carry on the ministry of Christ as his physical hands and feet today.

Reflection Questions

1. What are the strengths of the image of church as the body of Christ?

If Christ is the head, He is steering, making decisions and guiding.

2. How does your congregation act as the body of Christ? What are some of the ways you see your church committed to "seeking out the lost"?

Smumc has shown a lot of community outreach, there are a lot of ways to get involved. It seems a church of action.

3. Where do you see yourself fitting into the body?

I don't know! Outreach with kids.

Action Step

Use a concordance, or the keyword search at www.biblegateway.com, to look up "body of Christ." What other scripture verses do you find with this phrase? How do they add to your understanding of the nature of the church?

I Corin 12:12 all parts form one body
a body is one but made of many parts

Note

Moltmann, Jurgen. *The Church in the Power of the Spirit: A Contribution to Messianic Ecclesiology.* New York: Harper & Row, Publishers, Inc., 1977.

What Is the Church?:
Understanding Your Role in the Body

Day 5

Scripture Reading: Ephesians 4:11-16

So Christ himself gave the apostles, the prophets, the evangelists, the pastors and teachers, to equip his people for works of service, so that the body of Christ may be built up until we all reach unity in the faith and in the knowledge of the Son of God and become mature, attaining to the whole measure of the fullness of Christ.

Then we will no longer be infants, tossed back and forth by the waves, and blown here and there by every wind of teaching and by the cunning and craftiness of people in their deceitful scheming. Instead, speaking the truth in love, we will in all things grow up into him who is the head, that is, Christ. From him the whole body, joined and held together by every supporting ligament, grows and builds itself up in love, as each part does its work.

Insight

Personal trainers, sports coaches, and PE teachers will all tell you that to be truly fit, healthy, and coordinated, you have to take care of the entire body. A strong core benefits running, strong legs help support the back, and any kind of endurance training trims fat from the entire body. We hear over and over that "spot training," that is, training only a few muscles and ignoring the rest, is not effective for any athlete.

The same is true for the body of Christ. Each and every part of the body is essential, and when one part suffers, or is ignored, the whole body is less than it could be. You are a part of this body, and need to care for your own spiritual life. Like your physical diet, your spiritual diet will help nourish you. We need to take in a regular diet, such as worship, daily Scripture reading, study within

21

a small group. We are also fed by the presence of the community through our prayers and care for one another.

Just as knowledge is important in caring for our physical bodies, learning about your role in the body is also essential. Understanding what this role is, though, may not be immediately apparent. Maybe you see yourself more as an observer, as someone who comes and is fed by the community but does not play a vital role in the ministry. The truth, though, is that God has gifted you with skills and talents that can play an important role in building up others in the church, spreading the good news of God's love, and bringing healing to the world.

A healthy body requires regular exercise. A good diet and knowledge of how to care for the body are useless if they are never used. In the same way, preparing our minds for ministry and understanding our gifts and skills mean nothing if we do not put them to good use.

Our scripture passage today tells us that Christ equipped people so they can equip others in the community to become mature in faith, move toward unity, and help others grow, building them up in love. Being a member of a Christian community is important. It helps us grow individually and as a group. But there are also responsibilities that come when we become a member of the body of Christ.

As a different part of the body, we realize we have gifts to offer to that body and are called to use those gifts. This means that we are not fulfilling the commitment we made when we said, "I do," to the church if we are not using our gifts. In Ephesians 4:16, we discover that as the body of Christ, we are to grow and build ourselves up in love. But it says that this happens only when each part does its work within the body—the church.

What part of the body are you? What role is yours to play in the body of Christ? You may already know how God has gifted you. You may be using your gifts in your work, your home, another organization, or even the church. You may also have some undiscovered natural abilities. You now have the opportunity to discover how you might use these gifts as a member of the body of Christ in your local church.

The best way is simply to get involved. Do not wait to be asked. Instead look for a place where you think you could help. If you wait or procrastinate, you are missing opportunities. And the church is missing out on what you have to offer.

When you become an active part of the body of Christ, you help the church become fully what Christ intends, and when the church is unified and building people up in love, others will want to be a part of it also. In the end, this is what we are to be about as a church. We are to be a witness and a light reaching out to the world.

Reflection Questions

1. Think of your family or a close group of friends. When is a time that someone or some relationship within that circle was broken? How did it affect the whole group? Why is unity critical to the way a community functions together? *Cousin's wife. Focus shifts to her negativity instead of being together. Creates distinction.*

2. What are some ways that you are especially suited for serving God through the church? How will you exercise this gift? Who is someone you know who might be uniquely gifted but does not realize it? How can you affirm this person and his or her gift? *Cooking, organizing. Scott - by example.*

3. What does it mean to build up the church in love? How will you set aside your own desires as a member of the body of Christ to do this? What part of the work is yours to do? *To do for the church knowing it is for Christ & reflects Christ.*

Action Step

Make a list of your gifts and abilities. You may also want to ask a few people who know you well to make a list. As you look at your list(s), find one way to get involved at your church. Do not wait for someone to contact you. Take the first step and offer your help. You may not want to make a long-term commitment at this time, but instead try out a few things first.

Day 6

What Is the Church?:
How We Are the Church Together

Scripture Reading: 1 Corinthians 13

If I speak in human or angelic tongues, but do not have love, I am only a resounding gong or a clanging cymbal. If I have the gift of prophecy and can fathom all mysteries and all knowledge, and if I have a faith that can move mountains, but do not have love, I am nothing. If I give all I possess to the poor and give over my body [to hardship] that I may boast, but do not have love, I gain nothing.

Love is patient, love is kind. It does not envy, it does not boast, it is not proud. It does not dishonor others, it is not self-seeking, it is not easily angered, it keeps no record of wrongs. Love does not delight in evil but rejoices with the truth. It always protects, always trusts, always hopes, always perseveres.

Love never fails. But where there are prophecies, they will cease; where there are tongues, they will be stilled; where there is knowledge, it will pass away. For we know in part and we prophesy in part, but when completeness comes, what is in part disappears. When I was a child, I talked like a child, I thought like a child, I reasoned like a child. When I became a man, I put the ways of childhood behind me. For now we see only a reflection as in a mirror; then we shall see face to face. Now I know in part; then I shall know fully, even as I am fully known.

And now these three remain: faith, hope and love. But the greatest of these is love.

Insight

This passage on love is often read at weddings. Couples look to it as the ideal of what marital love should be like. It is the standard for a love that is committed and generous, that will see them through richer and poorer, in sickness and in health; and the passage works well for this purpose. It is also a great teaching for families, siblings, and friends to follow. Any relationship can benefit from learning to love like this.

It was originally written, though, not about romantic love or the love between friends, but about love that people shared within a community. The community to which it was written was struggling with loving one another. They had allowed petty bickering and power struggles to infect their community and compromise their ministry. You can imagine how they were treating one another by all the negative adjectives in this chapter; love is not envious, boastful, arrogant, or rude. If this is the way they were behaving toward one another, you can see why they were having problems. The first letter to the Corinthians, and especially this section, was written to remind them how they were to treat one another as they lived in community.

Sometimes church members do not love each other well. Maybe one member hurts another member's feeling so they lash out at each other, speaking harshly to each other in a committee meeting, and the negativity continues on from there. Quite often the problem stems from self-centeredness and pride. •

We are all uniquely gifted by God, and it is easy to think that what we have to contribute is more important than what someone else brings, or that our opinion counts for more, or that we are more valuable than those with so-called lesser gifts. This passage addresses this concern specifically, naming the gifts that were most valued in those times, prophecy, knowledge, faith, and says that they will all fade away, that they are worth nothing without love.

There will be times you will disagree with a sermon preached by your pastor, a resolution made by the church governance committee, or even the decision to change the soda machine from Pepsi to Coke products. Some conflict in the church will be normal. Stay focused on the vision and purpose of your church and what is truly important. Be willing to set aside your own needs, opinions, and desires for the good of the church.

How we love and care for one another in the family that is the church is both a reflection of our closeness with God and an example of God's love to those outside the church. People will be drawn to a community where people treat one another with kindness, respect, and patience, in large part because these qualities are so rare in our world. People go to work and face competition and an inhuman drive for efficiency and productivity. Often their families of origin are anything but peaceful and life-giving. If the church is, in contrast, a place that is affirming, loving, and giving, a place where they find peace, hope, and solace, then they will be open to hearing and experiencing God's presence. In fact, this may be our most effective means of spreading the good news of Jesus.

Reflection Questions

1. What is the vision and purpose of your church? What first drew you to this congregation? What kept you here?

   Relevancy to today, Congregation looks like it should — wide variety of people, everyone warm. Warmth, meaningful Sermons, opportunities to get involved

2. When the church frustrates or disappoints you (and it will), how will you react?

3. With which of the qualities of love in this scripture passage do you struggle the most? *Keeping records of wrong patience*

Action Step

Write down the vision and purpose of your church. What do you find most compelling about the vision and purpose statement? Schedule time with the pastor or other church leader to hear more about the vision and direction of the church so that if and when conflict arises you will be aware of what is most important to keep your church moving in the right direction.

What Is the Church?:
Saying Yes to Jesus

Scripture Reading: Acts 1:1-14

In my former book, Theophilus, I wrote about all that Jesus began to do and to teach until the day he was taken up to heaven, after giving instructions through the Holy Spirit to the apostles he had chosen. After his suffering, he presented himself to them and gave many convincing proofs that he was alive. He appeared to them over a period of forty days and spoke about the kingdom of God. On one occasion, while he was eating with them, he gave them this command: "Do not leave Jerusalem, but wait for the gift my Father promised, which you have heard me speak about. For John baptized with water, but in a few days you will be baptized with the Holy Spirit."

So when they met together, they asked him, "Lord, are you at this time going to restore the kingdom to Israel?"

He said to them: "It is not for you to know the times or dates the Father has set by his own authority. But you will receive power when the Holy Spirit comes on you; and you will be my witnesses in Jerusalem, and in all Judea and Samaria, and to the ends of the earth."

After he said this, he was taken up before their very eyes, and a cloud hid him from their sight.

They were looking intently up into the sky as he was going, when suddenly two men dressed in white stood beside them. "Men of Galilee," they said, "why do you stand here looking into the sky? This same Jesus, who has been taken from you into heaven, will come back in the same way you have seen him go into heaven."

Then the apostles returned to Jerusalem from the hill called the Mount of Olives, a Sabbath day's walk from the city. When they arrived, they went upstairs to the room where they were staying. Those present were Peter, John, James and Andrew; Philip and Thomas, Bartholomew and Matthew; James son of Alphaeus and Simon the Zealot, and Judas son of James. They all joined together constantly in prayer, along with the women and Mary the mother of Jesus, and with his brothers.

Insight

Waiting for a highly anticipated gift is rarely easy. I remember the summer of my first 10-speed bike. I was in third grade, old enough to run up the street to my friend's house by myself and even stay home alone for a few hours; and my parents had told me months before summer that it was time for me to have a bigger bike. They assured me they would buy me one for the summer, but they did not tell me specifically when that would happen. Every day I would come home and look for it, but I eventually had to learn to control my impatience while still maintaining excitement and hope for what awaited in the future.

The book of Acts is about the early days of the church, immediately following Jesus' resurrection. He spends 40 days with them, and then gives them parting instructions before ascending to heaven. The mission he gives to his disciples is to *"be [his] witnesses in Jerusalem, in all Judea and Samaria, and to the ends of the earth."* This is an exciting mission, but it is important to note that before this instruction Jesus tells them to wait.

The disciples are anxious for the fulfillment of all that Jesus promised, but he tells them to wait until they are filled with the power of the Holy Spirit. So, after Jesus leaves them, instead of immediately setting about their work, they gather in a room and commit themselves to prayer.

It is easy, especially in our culture, to get caught up in the busyness of life, church, faith, and relationships without first taking a pause to pray and to reflect. This pause is vital, though. If the disciples had not taken the time to wait and pray, they never would have received the promised power of the Holy Spirit (Acts 2:1-4), and the church would have died within a generation, if it ever got off the ground in the first place. If we do not take time for the holy pause in our lives, we will find ourselves jumping into work, even wholeheartedly and with great energy, that will ultimately not accomplish nearly what it could have had we waited and listened for God.

All Christians are given the gift of the Holy Spirit and can access the power of the Spirit to do God's work. They simply need to ask. Jesus says, *"If you. . .though you are evil, know how to give good gifts to your children, how much more will your Father in Heaven give the Holy Spirit to those who ask him!"* (Luke 11:13)

God very much wants to give us this gift, not only because of God's great love for us, but because God cares very much about the mission he has given us to be Christ's witnesses to the ends of the earth. We can only accomplish this through the power of the Holy Spirit. If we try to do so through our own power, we will fail.

So, will you say, "Yes"? Yes, to being a part of this new life in Christ? Yes, to being a part of the body of Christ? And yes, to being a part of God's redeeming work in the world? Saying "yes" is the first step of catching a new life.

Reflection Questions

1. What is the most difficult part about waiting on God's timing when we know the mission or goal? We want to go ahead on own timing.

2. When do you know the waiting is over and it is time to go out and work?

3. Have you ever directly asked God for the Holy Spirit?
   yes

Action Step

Take time for a simple prayer today. Ask God to give you the gift of the power of the Holy Spirit, direction as to how to use that power, and then clarity about the right time.

What Is the Church?:
Expecting the "Unexpected" in Saying, "I Do," to the Church

Scripture Reading: Acts 9:31

Then the church throughout Judea, Galilee and Samaria enjoyed a time of peace and was strengthened. Living in the fear of the Lord and encouraged by the Holy Spirit, it increased in numbers.

Insight

Families are important. We share meals together; help one another with projects; gather to celebrate holidays, birthdays, and anniversaries; vacation together; and sometimes simply sit and have conversation. Families are strengthened because of these times together. If a member of the family is not present, others often notice and miss that person's contribution.

Realizing that a young man had stopped attending church, one of our pastors made contact with him. He had attended for several years but then quit going, not because anything had offended him or because he no longer believed in God but because he felt that he had "learned everything" he needed to know and saw no reason to keep going. The strength of belonging to a church family that worshiped, grew, and served together never occurred to him.

Another conversation took place with a young couple who was married at the church. When the pastor talked about what their plan was for church involvement, they agreed with one another that church would be something they added to their lives after they had children. The pastor failed to convince them that adding church to their schedules after adding the complexity of children would be difficult if they were not already in the habit of attending. They saw no reason, though, to attend before children.

These three saw church mostly as a consumable convenience, there when they wanted something, forgettable when not needed. They did not understand church as a family, a community to which they could contribute. The joy of serving with a community that shares a common bond is amazing. By giving more, they could have lived fuller, richer lives.

What is even more amazing is how that bond reaches across congregational and denominational lines, so that all followers of Christ, of whatever creed, recognize one another as family members. I saw this reality at play in the fall of 2005, when the costliest and one of the strongest hurricanes in recorded history struck the Gulf Coast. Entire communities were completely devastated.

Our church quickly mobilized teams to respond. When our teams arrived, they soon noticed that they were not the first ones there. Several other vans and buses filled the street, and by the signs on the vehicles we saw that we were joining the Nazarenes, Catholics, Baptists, and Mormons. Though the havoc of the destruction was disheartening, the scene was a glimpse of the kingdom of God. The church group prepared and fed lunch to all of the workers. None of us even had to ask. Others had planned well and had brought plenty of the appropriate tools and resources so that our work was as efficient as possible. All contributed skills as well as sweat so that together we made a significant impact in the needs of that small region of the world. In our service, we forgot about doctrinal or style differences and remembered that we all serve the same God and live in the same needy world.

So what is the church? The church is the body of Christ doing what Christ would be doing if he were here physically on earth. Our understanding of church is greater when we recognize the fullness of the church universal, the church that includes every person who strives to follow Christ, no matter their religion, race, creed, political party, or personal opinions. That is not to say that none of our differences matter, for some are very important, but that ultimately we are part of the same family with millions of members.

Becoming a member of such a large family is one of the many unexpected blessings of saying "I do" to the church.

Reflection Questions

1. What unique blessing do you find in church that you would not find anywhere else? *Common faith, people seeking relationship w/ God.*

2. In what ways does your church participate and cooperate with other churches?

Outreach

3. How does understanding the church as a "family" shape your commitment? What excites you the most about the commitment you have made to serve Christ through the community of the church?

In a family, everyone has to do their part to keep the house running. Same with a church. We all need to do our part.

Action Step

Take time to learn about the distinctives of your particular church and/or denomination. Identify at least one friend, co-worker, or family member who belongs to a different kind of Christian church than you. Schedule some time with them for coffee or lunch, and ask about their faith and practices, what they love about their church, and the ways that their faith community serves God and the world.

Worship:
Being Fully Present

Scripture Reading: Romans 12:1-2

Therefore, I urge you, brothers and sisters, in view of God's mercy, to offer your bodies as a living sacrifice, holy and pleasing to God—this is true worship. Do not conform to the pattern of this world, but be transformed by the renewing of your mind. Then you will be able to test and approve what God's will is—his good, pleasing and perfect will.

Insight

We know that being present in worship is important. We dutifully set our alarms, get dressed, and go to church. We sit in the pew, stand when we are told, listen to the sermon, listen as the choir leads in singing, and may even give an offering when the plates are passed. Many times during worship, we find ourselves tired from a long week of work or from staying out too late the night before, distracted with thoughts of all the things on our to-do list, or critiquing the quality of the sermon. We are present, and our attendance has been checked off; but are we really *fully* present? Is simply being in the room what is required of us when we worship with our congregation, or is there something more?

A friend shared that she attended worship each Sunday morning. She was present and loved that she could just show up without investing anything of herself. Or at least this is what she thought at the time. Worship happened whether or not she was there because other people were responsible for it. She saw herself in the role of an audience member watching a performance. She saw the pastor and the musicians as the actual participants in worship. Although she may have never articulated it at the time, in hindsight she now sees that her understanding of being *present* in worship was misguided.

33

Danish philosopher and theologian Søren Kierkegaard affirms that this is a common conception amongst Christians, but he challenges us to think beyond it. Kierkegaard would have us understand pastors and musicians to be serving in a facilitating role. The active participants, in Kierkegaard's understanding of worship, are the members of the congregation. God is the audience.

If we understand worship in this way it is not enough for us simply to show up while we are overly tired and thinking about or focused on something else. We are called to come together as the body of Christ and to actively engage and worship God through the guidance and facilitation of pastors, leaders, and musicians. Worship is an act into which we are invited to perform, not a show that we are invited to attend.

Through this coming week we will be talking about and reflecting on worship in a variety of ways. We will talk about God as the center of our worship, the various elements of worship, preparing our hearts for worship both corporately and in our everyday lives, the activity of God in worship, and, finally, expecting the unexpected when we encounter the living God. In all of these ways we come together as members of the body of Christ as Paul said in his letter to the Romans, "*do not to conform to the pattern of this world, but be transformed by the renewing of [our] minds. Then [we] will be able to test and approve what God's will is—his good, pleasing and perfect will.*"

Worship can be a time of great joy and growth. We can experience God's love for us in worship. As we catch a new life, we can grow into who God would want us to be in worship. We can't, however, experience any of this if we do not show up and fully engage in the act of worship.

Reflection Questions

1. Think about the last time you were in worship. How did you understand your role? How did you understand the role of others?

   I looked at it more as going there to fill up and learn, not so much for God as the audience.

2. How does it change your understanding of worship to think of God as the audience and you as one of the active participants?

   Wow. Makes me want to really put love into my worship.

3. In what ways might you seek to be more fully present and engaged as you worship God?

Be more prayerful.

Action Step

You are not a consumer of worship, but rather an active participant in the act of praising God. As you worship with your local congregation this week, think intentionally and prayerfully about the role you play in that gathering. Picture God as the audience of your worship. Be intentional about being fully present in the act of worship.

Worship:
God Alone Is Worthy of our Worship

Day 10

Scripture Reading: Deuteronomy 5:6-8

"I am the LORD your God, who brought you out of Egypt, out of the land of slavery.

"You shall have no other gods before me.

"You shall not make for yourself an image in the form of anything in heaven above or on the earth beneath or in the waters below."

Insight

Living in bondage and slavery in Egypt, the Israelites were rescued by God. Even if you are relatively new to the Christian faith or to church you have likely seen the story of this rescue portrayed in film either in *The Ten Commandments* or in *The Prince of Egypt*. Coming out of Egypt, God, through Moses, gave the Israelites a series of laws to follow that were to govern their interactions with God and with the world. One of these laws (or commandments) was that the Israelites were to place no other gods above God—nothing that is in heaven above or the earth beneath.

I was recently standing at the customer service counter of a retail store waiting to return something. After standing in line for several minutes while other customers were helped, I stepped up to the counter. Just as the store employee greeted me he was interrupted mid-sentence by a ringing phone. He answered the phone and proceeded to help the customer on the line while I stood and waited for a good while longer. As I stood there I became increasingly frustrated by the fact I had been waiting and was present, but that something that was urgent and seemed more pressing had taken this employee's attention.

God must often feel this same way. We know that we need to spend time with God in prayer, that God wants us to live in certain ways, and that following God's commandments should be a priority, but there are often things that seem more pressing, making noise right in front of us and drawing our attention away from God.

We often do this with earthly things. We intend to spend time reading the Bible or praying each day, but pressing things at work or with our families become priorities. We know that we should give generously to support people in need in our communities, but the safety and security of our families and their future well-being consume the majority of our financial resources. We know that our hearts are what really matter to God, but we spend much more time each day preparing our hair, our clothing, and our appearance than we do preparing our hearts to encounter and to serve God in the world.

None of these things—work and family, preparing for the safety and well being of our loved ones' future, or taking care of our bodies—is inherently bad. However, when we begin to let them (individually or collectively) take priority over God in our lives, we have reason to be concerned.

In addition to these earthly things that can become priorities over God, it is worth taking just a minute to explore the reminder from Deuteronomy that we are not to make an idol of anything that is in heaven. Often Christians seem to be so focused on the afterlife that they begin to treat faith in Jesus as simply a way to get their ticket to heaven punched. It is important for us, as people of faith, never to idolize heaven so much that we forget our calling to live fully in this world and to help bring about the kingdom of God.

The very same saving love of God that worked to liberate the Israelites from bondage in Egypt seeks to work in our lives today. Let us always take the time and put forth the energy to make sure that we are investing fully in God's work in our life and not making an idol of anything else.

Reflection Questions

1. How have you experienced God's saving/freeing/liberating love?

When A was born, knowing she wald be OK.

2. What material things do you prioritize (or have you in the past prioritized) above God?

My schedule! Work, sleep, TV, etc.

3. What would it look like for you to live each day fully in God's presence as a response to God's saving love?

Probably a more purposeful day

Action Step

For the next week pay attention to the time that you spend physically getting ready for your day, including showering, shaving, picking out clothes, doing hair, putting on makeup, and brushing your teeth. Similarly, for the next week pay attention to the time that you spend spiritually getting ready for your day, including prayer, Bible study, and worship attendance. At the end of the week, think about changes that you might want to make or ways that you might hope to shift the balance between these two.

Worship:
Elements of Worship

Day 11

Scripture Reading: Acts 2:37-42

When the people heard this, they were cut to the heart and said to Peter and the other apostles, "Brothers, what shall we do?"

Peter replied, "Repent and be baptized, every one of you, in the name of Jesus Christ for the forgiveness of your sins. And you will receive the gift of the Holy Spirit. The promise is for you and your children and for all who are far off—for all whom the Lord our God will call."

With many other words he warned them; and he pleaded with them, "Save yourselves from this corrupt generation." Those who accepted his message were baptized, and about three thousand were added to their number that day.

They devoted themselves to the apostles' teaching and to fellowship, to the breaking of bread and to prayer.

Insight

True worship is God-centered. Our hearts are aligned with one purpose in mind—to worship God. When we worship, we are not concerned about the clothes we have on, whether we will be out in time for kickoff, or the roast that is in the oven. Worship includes several guiding elements, but the most important element is that our heart and attitude is in the right place.

Some elements to Christian worship are essential (though what those elements are would likely differ depending on who you ask). Today's scripture passage from the book of Acts contains instructions for new converts and includes the explanation that they *"devoted themselves to the apostles' teaching and to fellowship, to the breaking of bread and to prayer."*

For the first converts to the early church, the essential elements of worship were teaching, fellowship, communion, and prayer. While these have taken on various forms at different points in Christian history (and while they take various forms in different contexts today), they are all standards of Christian worship.

The teaching (or preaching) in our Christian worship is to be based on Scripture—the Old and New Testaments. In most Protestant churches this is the central act of worship and takes the most significant amount of time during the service. While some churches use technology in a variety of ways to supplement the teaching, the necessary element is some spoken exploration of how Scripture speaks to our human condition and who God would have us be in the midst of that reality.

While not often acknowledged or included as a formal element in worship services, fellowship continues to play a very important part in shaping and forming communities of faith. As we gather together with one another for worship each week, it is important that we come not only into God's presence but also into the presence of others who share our concerns about our greater community. As we grow into who God would have us be as individuals and as a community, we are then able to collectively respond to those needs.

In the last generation or two, many denominations served communion as infrequently as quarterly. Today many Protestant churches serve communion once a month. In some traditions communion is served weekly. In addition to the variance in frequency that exists, communion is served in many different ways (the two primary variations are dipping the bread into the cup, or eating a piece of bread and then drinking from the cup). Regardless of frequency or form, the significant thing is that people called Christians come together around a table to eat of a shared loaf and to drink of the cup to remember Christ's sacrifice and our call to be the body of Christ in the world.

Finally, prayer is the act that is to undergird all of our work together as the church, but it also plays a special role in corporate worship. Some churches still share joys and concerns each week, while others have a time of prayer led by the preacher or another pastor. Some allow time for silent prayer and confession, and others have their prayers well scripted with very little time for silence. As we go to God in prayer during worship, we have the awesome opportunity to connect with the creator of the universe in an intimate and personal way. It is one of the greatest joys we can experience as people of faith.

These four elements of worship are by no means exhaustive, but you will likely find them all in most mainline Protestant worship services. These elements help lead us and prepare our hearts as we encounter the living God.

Reflection Questions

1. What elements of worship speak to you the most? What is it about them that help you connect with God?

   teaching - I love to learn. and understanding how scripture relates to us is relevant & helpful

2. Are there worship elements that are absolutely non negotiable for you; things that you must experience to feel as if you have worshiped? What are these elements, and why do they feel like must-haves?

   hymns. I really enjoy singing them, some are so moving and emotional.

3. Reflect on a time that you have experienced the tension between worship feeling like more of a performance for you to observe than something to which you were invited to participate? What elements added to this tension? *Alan's funeral*

Action Step

As you reflect on your experience of worship, note the expectations you bring. How do these expectations affect your participation? Do any of these expectations take your focus away from making God the center of your worship? Make a commitment that in your experience of worship, your number one expectation will be to encounter the living God.

1/18

Day 12

Worship:
Preparing Our Hearts for Corporate Worship

Scripture Reading: 2 Samuel 6:1-5, 12-15

David again brought together all the able young men of Israel—thirty thousand. He and all his men went to Baalah in Judah to bring up from there the ark of God, which is called by the Name, the name of the LORD Almighty, who is enthroned between the cherubim on the ark. They set the ark of God on a new cart and brought it from the house of Abinadab, which was on the hill. Uzzah and Ahio, sons of Abinadab, were guiding the new cart with the ark of God on it, and Ahio was walking in front of it. David and the whole house of Israel were celebrating with all their might before the LORD, with castanets, harps, lyres, timbrels, sistrums and cymbals. . .

Now King David was told, "The LORD has blessed the household of Obed-Edom and everything he has, because of the ark of God." So David went to bring up the ark of God from the house of Obed-Edom to the City of David with rejoicing. When those who were carrying the ark of the LORD had taken six steps, he sacrificed a bull and a fattened calf. Wearing a linen ephod, David was dancing before the LORD with all his might, while he and the entire house of Israel were bringing up the ark of the LORD with shouts and the sound of trumpets.

Insight

The first time I attended a Kansas City Chief's football game I went into culture shock. *Fanatic* does not even begin to describe the typical person at a Chief's game. Hours before the game, thousands of people gather in the parking lot to enjoy tailgating. Smoke billows into the sky from all of the barbeque grills, the smell of grilling brats and hamburgers fills the air, and the atmosphere is electric. People mingle between cars getting to know new

42

friends, sharing food, and swapping stories. As people enter the stadium there is a feeling of anticipation. Soon the stadium is filled with tens of thousands of people dressed in red and white, trying to get as close to the front as possible, standing on their feet, jumping up and down, clapping their hands, and yelling as loudly as they can. People I know to be respectable members of society, including my senior pastor, act with unbridled passion and devotion, and this is all before the game even starts.

Contrast that to another gathering played out across the country each weekend. People gather for worship, slowly shuffling to find seats in the back of the room, arms crossed, very few people talking to their neighbor. In fact, a large number did not even arrive before the service but instead entered the sanctuary ten or fifteen minutes after the start of the service. They stand for singing, but barely make a sound. Some of these people may have been the same ones who the night before attended and fully participated in a high school, college, or professional sporting event. I wonder what happened to their hearts and their passion between the game and the worship service.

King David was called a man after God's own heart. He was not the most moral or upright man. He committed adultery and murder and was prone to wrath and violence, yet he loved God with all his heart. In fact, he was known for his passionate, unfettered worship of God. In this passage from 2 Samuel, David is celebrating the return of the ark of the covenant to the Israelites from their enemies. The ark was a physical representation of the presence of God. David was excited about bringing the ark to Jerusalem, the capital city and home to his palace, because it signified that Israel was under God's rule and protection, that the Lord was the true king, and that David was his handpicked servant. He was so excited, in fact, that he acted in a completely undignified manner, as his wife later pointed out to him. He danced in the streets like a commoner, not worried even about what he was wearing.

When we gather for worship as a community of faith, it is a time of great celebration. We are welcoming the very presence of God. Like the football fans, when we arrive early with anticipation, it affects the spirit of the entire experience. Like David, when we let go of our assumed facades and inhibitions, we are able to bring to our worship our whole hearts, bodies, and spirits, so that God may do great things through us. And though, as we shall see tomorrow, there is a time and a place for individual worship, there is something important about worshiping with a community. When we lift our voices together, sharing a common space and a common meal with one another, we can experience with greater intensity the fire of God's spirit. We can learn from, inspire, and encourage one another. God can speak to a people a vision that is more difficult to hear as individuals.

This is why corporate worship is essential to the Christian life. It is not something we do merely out of obligation, but it is an opportunity to experience God in a way that we cannot experience anywhere else.

Reflection Questions

1. What is a corporate experience, worship or otherwise, where you have experienced great passion, enthusiasm, and participation by those who attended? What is one thing you could do in worship to engage more fully? *Kickoff, training. Sit with others who engage fully.*

2. In which part of the worship service do you most connect with God? With others? *Hymns, sharing of the peace.*

3. What keeps you from attending worship weekly? What do you need to do to adjust your schedule and priorities to make weekly worship a priority? *too many other obligations, things to get done.*

Action Step

This coming weekend, arrive at worship at least ten minutes early. Spend that time preparing for worship by taking a few minutes to pray, finding someone you do not know and talking with them, reading the Scripture lesson for that week, walking around the sanctuary and taking note of the details you had not noticed before, or simply sitting and allowing your spirit to settle in to that time and place.

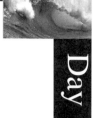

Worship:
Preparing Our Hearts for Everyday Worship

Scripture Reading: Psalm 8

Lord, our Lord, how majestic is your name in all the earth! You have set your glory above the heavens.

Through the praise of children and infants you have established a stronghold against your enemies, to silence the foe and the avenger.

When I consider your heavens, the work of your fingers, the moon and the stars, which you have set in place,

what are mere mortals that you are mindful of them, human beings that you care for them?

You have made them a little lower than the heavenly beings and crowned them with glory and honor.

You made them rulers over the works of your hands; you put everything under their feet:

all flocks and herds, and the animals of the wild,

the birds in the sky, and the fish in the sea, all that swim the paths of the seas.

Lord, our Lord, how majestic is your name in all the earth!

Insight

My friend Dagney, who helped contribute to the writing of this devotion book, shares that her 5-year-old is full of questions, one of her all time favorites being, "Mommy, how did God make. . ." This question offers endless variety, from how did God make trees, bugs, dirt, and birds to how did God make cars, buildings, roads, and chairs. Her inspiration for the question is usually what is right in front of her at the moment. She sees something, she

Catch a New Life

wonders about it, and she wants to understand how it is connected with God. Dagney tries to answer the questions about natural objects by breaking them down into smaller elements as much as possible, "God makes birds out of bones, feathers, muscles, and blood." The manufactured objects stumped her for a while, but then she came up with an answer that satisfied her daughter, "God made people, and people made the road."

What I love about the questions Dagney's daughter is asking is that she looks for God everywhere in everyday objects. When we look at the world through her eyes, we too begin to see the mark of God in everything around us: the air we breathe, the food we eat, the grass beneath our feet, the faces of others around us, and even roads, buildings, and cars. With this in mind, we remember to take a moment to offer a word of thanks and praise to God, listening for God's voice through these, striving to be still and feel God's presence even if only for a second or two. These little reminders throughout the day can keep us in constant communion, constant worship with God. We give thanks, we admire God, we ask God to continue to walk with us, and we hear the call of God's voice. The days where we do not remember to pause and appreciate God's presence in everything, aiming to be in continuous worship, are more difficult and tedious, and robbed of a certain amount of joy.

The psalmist, too, recognizes God's handiwork in creation, praising, "*the work of [God's] fingers, the moon and the stars which [God has] set in place.*" The psalmist takes time to pause, to consider the surroundings, and to reflect upon what these communicate about the presence and nature of God. God is greater than we can imagine, always and everywhere before us.

The psalmist then goes on to celebrate how our relationship with God determines our relationship with the rest of creation. Although we seem so very small and insignificant compared with what God has done, God has crowned us "*with glory and honor*," and given all of creation over to our care and stewardship.

As we worship God in our everyday life, we are reminded of how close we are to God's heart as well as the immense responsibility God has given us. We are to love as God loves, and our worship, our relationship with God, invites us to learn how to do this. Our everyday worship, changes us little by little, so that we fall more in love with God and grow into the role for which God has designed us as God's children, co-creators, friends, and objects of God's love.

46

Reflection Questions

1. Is there a place or a time where you most intensely feel the presence of God? *When I am in a beautiful outdoor space or witnessing some kind of creature.*

2. What obstacles hinder you from taking moments in your day to look for, appreciate, and love God?

   life: kids, work, house

3. How do you think God views you?

Action Step

In the next day, take at least three opportunities to stop what you are doing, look around you, say a word of thanks, and recognize at least one object of beauty that points back to God.

Worship:
The Activity of God in Worship

Scripture Reading: Matthew 11:28-30

"Come to me, all you who are weary and burdened, and I will give you rest. Take my yoke upon you and learn from me, for I am gentle and humble in heart, and you will find rest for your souls. For my yoke is easy and my burden is light."

Insight

We each have a different experience of worship. For some, attending worship services as a child was miserable. The thought may conjure up memories of getting into trouble for not being quiet enough or for fidgeting. For others who were older, worship may have become a place where they felt like they were not measuring up; they may have left each week feeling more miserable about themselves. You may have had a similar experience. You may have kept attending because it was what you thought you were "supposed" to do, but without experiencing the life-giving power of what worship is meant to be, or you may have simply stopped attending altogether and are now taking a new step.

I personally am one who has attended worship my entire life, but it was only in recent years that I heard the idea of approaching worship with the expectation of encountering God. It is God who invites us into worship, not to make our lives miserable, but rather to give us love and blessing, to deepen God's relationship with us.

Jesus' disciples saw God when they looked at Jesus. To spend time with him was to spend time with God. So, when Jesus gave instructions on how they were to be in relationship with him, this was also instruction as to how they were to be in relationship with the God they had worshiped their whole lives. In contrast to the teachings of the religious leaders of the time, who wanted the people to fear them and fear God so that they could control the people, Jesus taught that God's desire was that God's people approach as children, laying down their burdens and finding rest, solace, and healing in God's presence.

Every element of worship can serve to bring us closer to God, to give us an opportunity to experience God. One of the elements where this is most visible is in communion. Our lay leaders who serve communion find great joy in this task, as one shared with me recently. After attending a class where we taught about the sacraments, he asked to join the team that helped serve communion. The next time I saw him, he approached me with a big smile and sparkling eyes, "It was even better than I expected," he said, "to look in people's faces as they received the bread. I can't describe how wonderful it is." He was delighting in actively participating in God's grace. He could see in the faces of worshipers that they were truly experiencing rest for their souls as they came forward and received the common meal that is the body of Christ.

Although Jesus promises rest, he does say there is a yoke to bear. The word *yoke* here indicates the teaching that a disciple of a teacher would follow. Jesus is telling his disciples that there will be an expectation for how to live; but unlike the leaders and teachers who set forth unreasonable, heavy, life-stealing requirements, Jesus' teaching is life-giving and refreshing for those who follow. Jesus' passion is to bring peace, joy, and restoration to people. This is the activity of God in our worship.

Reflection Questions

1. If you went to church growing up, what was your experience like?

   n/a

2. Which heavy burdens would you want to lay down before God in worship? the need to simplify my life + help to determine a career

3. Can you think of a time when you have experienced healing or cleansing in worship? 1ˢᵗ time @ St. Marks, at BSF

Action Step

On a piece of paper, write down any burdens that you would like to lay down. Pray over each one, asking God to help you let go of them. The next time you go to worship, take time before or during the service to pray over the list again, then rip it into several pieces and throw them away as you leave.

Worship:
Expecting the Unexpected in Worship

Scripture Reading: Revelation 4:10-11

The twenty-four elders fall down before him who sits on the throne and worship him who lives for ever and ever. They lay their crowns before the throne and say:

"You are worthy, our Lord and God, to receive glory and honor and power, for you created all things, and by your will they were created and have their being."

Insight

Yes, I will admit for the sake of a metaphor, I was homecoming queen of the mighty, fighting Aurora Houn Dawgs. I will never forget the feeling of wearing the crown on my head. I must admit it felt good, and I felt pretty important. I remember arriving home after the final dance and taking off the crown, setting it aside on my dresser never to put it on again, but having the feeling of wearing it linger. Although I never physically wore that crown again, I have continued to wear many crowns over the course of my life.

We have been considering what it means to worship God corporately as a member of the body of Christ in the church and also individually. Let's take a step back and define worship. The word *worship* comes from the old English *worth-ship*, which means to ascribe worth or value to something or someone. In both Hebrew and Greek, there are two major kinds of words for worship. The first means to bow down, to kneel, and to put one's face down as an act of respect and submission. Such body language says, "I will do whatever you want me to. I am ready to listen to your instructions, and I am willing to obey." The other means to serve. It carries the idea of doing something for God—making a sacrifice or carrying out God's instructions.

The scene played out in today's scripture verses is powerful. The elders have declared God as "*holy, holy, holy,*" and as they approach the throne of God their only response is to fall down on their knees, throwing their crowns aside. Many of us enter worship each week physically but have yet to lay aside all those little crowns we wear on our heads. We know that God should be center of our lives and should be the only one sitting on the throne, but still we continue to wrestle God off. Sometimes we do so knowingly, and other times not so knowingly.

We make other things the objects of our worship. We ascribe worth to our jobs, our busy schedules, our children, our possessions, our hobbies, and our pride. We create our own kingdoms, seeking first our own plans, wants, and desires versus seeking first the kingdom of God. And, we cannot seem to lay aside our crowns of self-centeredness, self-dependence, fear, or just plain laziness.

The elders were clear on the object of their worship: "*our Lord and God.*" They continued, "*You are worthy to receive glory and honor and power, for you created all things, and by your will they were created and have their being.*" When we worship God, we acknowledge God's glory, honor, and power. We do so through singing, praying, preaching, participating in Holy Communion, giving, and serving.

One of my favorite hymns is "How Great Thou Art," which begins with the phrase, "O, Lord, my God, when I in awesome wonder." That understanding is what we need to reclaim in our worship—awe and wonder in the presence of God. Through worship, you are invited to join the elders as we gather together for worship in praising God. You are invited into the throne room to experience the presence of the living God. Through your worship, you can expect what might have been unexpected before—that you are encountering the living God, a God that is up close and personal, not far off in the distance.

With such knowledge, how can you declare anything other than, "God, you are Holy and I am your humble servant"?

Reflection Questions

1. What does the word *worship* mean? To what do you ascribe worth? Make a list. To attibute worth a value to something or someone. My family, my stuff,

52

2. What crowns are you wearing that need to be set aside? What makes this difficult? *Self dependence. My ego.*

3. How will your experience of worship be different knowing that worship is being invited into the living presence of God? What do you need to do to reclaim awe and wonder of God? *Leave everything else outside of the sanctuary.*

Action Step

Participation in worship and preparing your heart each week for worship is important. Here are a few suggestions:

1. Arrive early so that you are not rushed.
2. Invite the presence of God into your worship experience, and expect that God will be there.
3. Sing songs of praise to God. Do not worry about those sitting next to you. Pay attention to the words of the songs and how they speak to you.
4. Enter into the corporate prayer time not as an observer but as an active participant.
5. As you listen to the sermon, ask that God will speak to you. Listen for what God is trying to teach you.
6. Be prepared to respond. This may take many different forms. It may be in your offering, deciding to serve, reconciling a broken relationship, or making a change in a destructive behavior. And it may simply be to go out and be silent, quietly reflecting on God's work in your life.

Growing Spiritually:
The Goal of Spiritual Growth

Scripture Reading: 2 Corinthians 3:17-18

Now the Lord is the Spirit, and where the Spirit of the Lord is, there is freedom. And we all, who with unveiled faces contemplate the Lord's glory, are being transformed into his image with ever-increasing glory, which comes from the Lord, who is the Spirit.

Insight

Remember Ebenezer Scrooge? Long before Dr. Seuss brought the Grinch into being, Charles Dickens created Ebenezer Scrooge, who played a prominent role in *A Christmas Carol.* Scrooge taught the English-speaking world to exclaim, "Bah! Humbug!" He was, said Dickens, "a squeezing, wrenching, grasping, scraping, clutching, covetous old sinner! Hard and sharp as flint, from which no steel had ever struck out generous fire; secret, and self-contained, and solitary as an oyster. The cold within him froze his old features. . .and spoke out shrewdly in his grating voice."

But he changed. Oh, how he changed! By the end of the story, Ebenezer Scrooge was giving away coins, buying the biggest turkey in the butcher's window for poor Bob Cratchit and his family, promising to care for the crippled Tiny Tim, and smiling at everyone he met. "He became as good a friend, as good a master, and as good a man, as the good old city knew, or any other good old city, town or borough, in the good old world." And all it took was one long, long night spent with the ghosts of Christmas Past, Christmas Present, and Christmas Future!

You have set out on a journey even bigger and better than Ebenezer Scrooge's journey—the journey of spiritual growth. It can start any time, not just at Christmas. You will have better company on your journey than Scrooge did—today's scripture verse says that God's Holy Spirit is your guide and companion. Your goal takes in all the good things that happened to Scrooge, but reaches far beyond them. For our verse today says the goal of spiritual growth is nothing less than being transformed into the image of the Lord Jesus Christ!

That is one reason this journey takes more than a single night. We need a lot of transforming before we become anything similar to the image of Christ. It is a lifelong process, or, as our text puts it, a journey filled "with ever-increasing glory," as we keep moving toward our goal.

An even bigger reason our journey is a lifelong quest is that God does not simply hand us character on a silver platter. Here is how the apostle Paul described the pathway that develops character in us: "*We also glory in our sufferings, because we know that suffering produces perseverance; perseverance, character; and character, hope. And hope does not put us to shame, because God's love has been poured out into our hearts through the Holy Spirit, who has been given to us*" (Romans 5:3-5).

Peter gives a similar pattern for character building: "*For this very reason, make every effort to add to your faith goodness; and to goodness, knowledge; and to knowledge, self-control; and to self-control, perseverance; and to perseverance, godliness; and to godliness, mutual affection; and to mutual affection, love. For if you possess these qualities in increasing measure, they will keep you from being ineffective and unproductive in your knowledge of our Lord Jesus Christ*" (2 Peter 1:5-8).

The apostle Paul summed up spiritual growth in these words: "*Therefore, my dear friends, as you have always obeyed. . .continue to work out your salvation with fear and trembling, for it is God who works in you to will and to act in order to fulfill his good purpose*" (Philippians 2:12-13). There is work for each of us to do—we "*make every effort*," as Peter put it—but we are not doing any of it on our own, because God works in each of us. In the next seven devotions, you will discover certain key steps to take for spiritual growth. But this is not a self-improvement program. The steps we take to catch a new life are ways to open our hearts and lives so that God's power can work to change us from the inside out.

The goal of spiritual growth is transformation into nothing less than the image of Jesus Christ. And there is no greater journey any of us can ever make.

Through this journey, you will find that God's power will change you deeply, and for the better.

Reflection Questions

1. In what ways did you sense God at work in you as you made your decision to join the church? In what sense did you have to make a choice for yourself? *Sense of happiness, feeling at home.*

   There really wasn't a choice to make for me.

2. What good things do you anticipate and hope for as you set out on this journey of spiritual growth? What, if anything, concerns you, or do you fear may be difficult in the course of your journey?

   Spiritual growth & hope for meeting my family.
   Concern: overextending myself. :-

3. "Where the Spirit of the Lord is, there is freedom." In what part of your inner life do you particularly yearn for freedom?

Action Step

Take a piece of paper, and create two columns. Title the first column "My Life Before Christ." In this column, list the qualities and actions that you have already left behind, or that you believe God is calling you to leave behind. Title the second column "My New Life in Christ." List here the positive qualities and actions that you anticipate working with God to make real in your life as you journey forward in spiritual growth. You may want to keep this paper with you all week as your study and prayer trigger new ideas.

Growing Spiritually:
Reading the Bible

Scripture Reading: Acts 17:11-12

Now the Berean Jews were of more noble character than those in Thessalonica, for they received the message with great eagerness and examined the Scriptures every day to see if what Paul said was true. Many of them believed, as did also a number of prominent Greek women and many Greek men.

Insight

Did you ever try to assemble a bicycle, set up a new cell phone, or start running a complicated software program? A lot of us want to dive in, so all we ask is, "How do I start?" And off we go—until we come to that point where we cannot figure out something essential. Usually it is only then that we reach for the instruction sheet, try the online help, or open the operator's manual.

Many of us approach life the same way. We dive in, try various approaches, get stuck at times, squirm out of the tight spots, and keep going. Sometimes we do not look for help or direction until we are up against a dead-end. We know something essential is missing, but we cannot seem to find it.

There is a crucial source of strength and help for your Christian journey—the Bible. Christians across the centuries would probably recommend reading the Bible more than any other practice for those who are serious about growing as followers of Jesus. We have the inspiring example of the early believers in the city of Berea described in today's Bible verses. They read Scripture daily to confirm the truth of what they were learning. They knew this was a central resource for their spiritual growth.

Of course, your Bible is not much like bicycle assembly instructions or a

57

software manual. Many people expect it to be. They think the Bible is a kind of spiritual encyclopedia, a reference book. If they have a question about ethics (taxes, perhaps?), they would like to be able to look in the index under "T" and find a verse or two that answers their question. Reference books are a list of entries, all of roughly equal value and accuracy. Using the Bible like a reference book can cause a lot of trouble. On many subjects, persons with differing understandings can each find two or three verses somewhere in the Bible that seem to uphold their view. We argue, we each quote verses, nothing gets settled, each of us is sure the other one does not really believe the Bible, and no one grows spiritually. That is what some people picture when we talk about reading the Bible, and they often think, "Maybe I'll just skip that."

But the Bible is a collection of 66 books, letters, and other types of literature, written over roughly 1200 to 1500 years. Put all those pieces together, and you find that more than anything else the Bible is a story. Now a story is not a reference book, and you do not read it the same way. Stories have peaks and valleys, side plots and soaring main lines, heroes and villains. Once we know the story, we may turn to a favorite line somewhere in chapter 7, but we understand that line in terms of how it fits into the whole story. The Bible is the story of how God has related to human beings in many times and cultures. When we read it as a story, its epic sweep and sometimes shocking honesty take our breath away and set us thinking deeply about our own life. We start learning to recognize where God appears in our own story, the places where the veil between our world and God's world stretches so thin that it disappears.

One more thing: Christians believe God inspired all of the 40 or so writers of the Bible. The Bible is not merely human thinking (though it certainly reflects that in many places)—it is God's message to us. So to get the full richness of the story, we need to immerse ourselves in it in such a way as to attempt to become part of the narrative. That's why three different authors (Jeremiah 15:16, Ezekiel 3:1-3, and Revelation 10:9-10) all used the same vivid image. Confronted by a scroll that represented God's word, they all talked about "eating" the book.

What they were trying to tell us is that we read the Bible not just for information but for transformation. When we get inside the Bible and the Bible gets inside of us, God can work through all of the teachings and laws and stories to shape us into transformed people.

Reflection Questions

1. How much do you know about the Bible? What assumptions do you make about the truthfulness of its spiritual message? *Quite a bit.*

   That we can't comprehend everything about God and the bible helps us to learn & understand on our level.

2. Who have you known who read the Bible a lot? What effects, positive or negative, did you see that have in that person's life? How has that affected your attitude toward reading the Bible?

3. Does it make sense to you to distinguish between a reference book and a story? Which approach to the Bible have you seen the most of? Have you ever read for yourself the story of Jesus, as told by Matthew, Mark, Luke, and John? (These books, located in the New Testament are a great place to start!) *Yes! Story with reference*

Action Step

Familiarize yourself with the books of the Bible. Examine your Bible's table of contents, noting the order in which the books occur. Page through the Bible several times, noting the longer and shorter books. Note the relative proportions of the Old Testament (also known as the Hebrew scriptures) and the New Testament.

Growing Spiritually:
Tools for Reading the Bible

Day 18

Scripture Reading: 2 Timothy 2:14-15

Keep reminding God's people of these things. Warn them before God against quarreling about words; it is of no value, and only ruins those who listen. Do your best to present yourself to God as one approved, a worker who does not need to be ashamed and who correctly handles the word of truth.

Insight

"Wear a seatbelt." "Don't go too fast." "Stay on your side of the road." When parents hand their child the keys to the car, they usually want to pass on words of instruction. And with good reason. Correctly handled, a car is a wonderful thing. Wrongly used, it can become a destructive force that hurts people, including the driver.

In today's reading, the apostle Paul sounds like a proud, cautious dad handing Timothy the keys. In a sense, he was. Second Timothy may well be the last letter Paul wrote before the Romans executed him. Timothy was a beloved protégé of Paul's, as close to a son as the proudly unmarried old missionary ever had. And Paul was handing off not the keys to a car but the "keys" to his ministry to the youthful Christian congregations of Asia Minor. "Timothy," he says, "be sure you correctly handle the word of truth."

As we discovered yesterday, we, too, want to read the Bible in the right ways. We want it to help us grow spiritually. Happily, there are tools to help us do that. Let's briefly review a few of the most important ones.

- Translations

    Different parts of the Bible were written in Hebrew, Aramaic, and

Greek. Unless you are fluent in those three languages, you will need a good English translation of the Bible. Here is the good news: there are many excellent translations available. You may want to ask your pastor or some trusted Christian friends to recommend a favorite. The key is to find a translation you will read and to read it, regularly.

Today we have great Web sites that give access to many English translations, making comparisons much easier. You may want to check out www.biblegateway.com or www.youversion.com. They can deepen and enrich your Bible reading.

- Study Bibles

   You will probably want to ground yourself in the Bible's story by getting a good study Bible that uses whichever translation you have found to be most readable. A study Bible, in addition to the text of the Bible, contains notes that explain key ideas or puzzling historical references in the text, along with introductory articles, maps, and other aids to understanding the Bible's story. Some study Bibles offer direct cues on how to apply what the Bible says; others simply explain the background of the text and let you and the Holy Spirit work out the application to your life.

   There are many excellent study Bibles. Four of the most-often recommended are the *New Interpreter's Study Bible*, the *TNIV Study Bible*, the *Life Application Study Bible*, or the *Harper-Collins Study Bible*. As with a translation, find a study Bible whose layout and approach work well for you, drawing you into the Bible's story and helping you understand what you read without too much effort. If you already own a Bible you like, you can get most of the same study aids that a study Bible offers by buying a Bible handbook.

- Other Tools

   –Bible dictionary. The articles in a Bible dictionary are typically more extensive than the helps in a study Bible, and often cover a wider range of topics.

   –Bible commentaries. In a commentary, a scholar leads you through a book of the Bible almost verse-by-verse to give you greater understanding of the issues and situations the book addresses. William

61

Barclay's *Daily Study Bible* series blends wide historical knowledge of the Greek and Roman world with reflections on how we can live as faithful Christians. More recently Tom Wright has written a similar series called *The New Testament for Everyone*. Just be careful not to let reading a commentary take the place of reading the Bible itself.

–Read-through-the-Bible reading program. There are several online resources or books available at your local Christian bookstore that offer guided programs to help you read through the Bible in a specified length of time, often one year.

–Hymnal or worship song book. Many song and hymn lyrics are taken directly from Scripture.

The goal of reading the Bible is to allow God's word to speak to us. Tools help in gaining additional information and perspectives from others. It is tempting to say, "I don't read the Bible because I simply don't understand it." It is easy to get caught up in this excuse, and yes, sometimes Scripture is difficult to understand. But keep at it!

Just like a father desires a relationship with his children, your heavenly Father is reaching out through Scripture to build a relationship with you. The Bible is a collection of writings to let you know how much God loves you. As you read them over and over using whatever tools you select, allow the words to penetrate your heart.

Reflection Questions

1. What are some of the key "tools" you use in your profession or daily work? How important is it to your effectiveness that you have good tools to work with? Can you see how the same is true of Bible study?

   Databases. Very important, yes.

2. What do you believe it means to rightly handle the word of truth? Have you ever seen the Bible mishandled? If so, how did that affect your trust in the Bible's message? *Yes – doesn't affect my trust on the bible, just messenger.*

3. Paul cautions Timothy against getting caught up in quarreling or arguing.

How can you focus your Bible study on hearing God's word for your life, rather than debating with other Christians? What are the spiritual benefits of avoiding fruitless quarrels? *Have always tried.*

Action Step

Once you have obtained a study Bible, or a Bible handbook to use with your Bible, set aside time to get to know its various features. Notice how the study notes are arranged (and if there are different types of notes), where the maps are located, any lists of key words or verses, where introductory notes or explanatory essays are placed, and what kinds of information they are designed to give you. As you would with any important pursuit, get to know your tools and how to use them most effectively. Find a way to stay motivated.

Growing Spiritually:
Prayer

Scripture Reading: Luke 11:1-4

One day Jesus was praying in a certain place. When he finished, one of his disciples said to him, "Lord, teach us to pray, just as John taught his disciples."

He said to them, "When you pray, say: " 'Father, hallowed be your name, your kingdom come.

Give us each day our daily bread.

Forgive us our sins, for we also forgive everyone who sins against us. And lead us not into temptation.'"

Insight

You want to grow spiritually. You are serious about catching a new life, becoming a transformed person, growing more and more like Jesus. It is great that you have the opportunity to belong to a church family, getting support, encouragement, and wisdom from others who are making this journey with you. It is a wonderful thing to have the Bible and to be able to weave the principles of its grand story of God's relationship with human beings into the fabric of your life. Still, wouldn't it be awesome if you could talk directly with God about your growth, asking help with your struggles, sharing your joy in the steps forward that you take, and having God guide you as you grow?

You can! Prayer plays this role in spiritual growth. Of course, the word *prayer* does not always bring this to mind. Depending on your background and experiences, you may think *prayer* means listening to a pastor or relative drone through a repetitive batch of lifeless phrases in Old English. You may think "prayer" means using the right set of "magic" words that God demands but that do not seem to have much connection to your everyday life. You may think *prayer* is limited to four subjects—relatives' illnesses, church activities, confessing what you've done wrong, and asking for noble things like world peace—with everything else out of bounds.

In fact, *prayer* simply means communicating with God. It's not a one-size-fits-all exercise. There is not one right way to pray. Jesus' disciples saw him praying, often and in many different circumstances. As we see in today's Bible reading, they asked him to teach them how to have the same kind of communication with God. Jesus did not respond by telling them he was special and they could not possibly talk with God the way he did. He did not give them an elaborate, complicated prayer, filled with fancy words. Instead, he seemed to say rather matter-of-factly, "Sure—here's a model for how you can pray." (You may be more familiar with the slightly longer version of this prayer recorded in Matthew 6:9-13.)

If you have ever heard a magnificent, eloquent prayer in a worship service and thought, "I can't pray like that," be assured—you do not have to! The essence of prayer is simply honestly communicating to God whatever is on your heart, which is not limited only to requests. Pastor and author Brian McLaren suggests that one way to grasp the essence of prayer is to reduce prayers to one word, such as "Thanks," "Sorry," "Help," "Please," "Wow," and "Why?" Thinking about how you communicate in other close relationships may help you come up with other one-word prayers you will want to add to this list.

Thinking about how communication patterns in other relationships will also remind you of another often-overlooked aspect of prayer: listening. Listening to God, however, is different from listening to one of your friends. We listen to God not so much with our ears as with our mind and our heart. (According to the Bible, God seldom—though not never—speaks to us in an audible voice.) God can reach us more directly than our human friends can. As you walk with God, you will learn to "listen" for distinctive inner impressions, ideas, and promptings—what my senior pastor calls "nudges"—from God. Of course, not every impulse you have comes from God. That is in part why you need the Bible—to help you understand more clearly the types of nudges God is likely to send you. But learning to listen is a vital part of a strong prayer life.

Reflection Questions

1. How, if at all, have you experienced prayer up to now? What type of role has it played in your life?

   sporadic

2. For what reasons do you think Jesus prayed as regularly as he did? What does his example suggest to you about the role prayer can play in your spiritual growth?

   More important than I make it.

3. Think about a friend you have met in the last five years. How did you get to know the person? What helped the friendship to grow? What does that experience tell you about how you can grow closer to God through prayer?

   Spending time together

Action Step

One of the simplest forms of prayer, practiced by God's people through the centuries, is the breath prayer. A breath prayer is a simple phrase, short enough to be repeated with a single breath. A few examples are:

Come to me, Lord Jesus.
Guide me, O God.
Lord Jesus, have mercy.

Choose a breath prayer. If necessary, write it on a small card and put it where you will see it regularly during the day. Whenever you have a spare moment, and particularly at moments of tension or stress during your day, inwardly (or in a soft voice, if the setting allows) repeat your breath prayer. Make notes of how this prayer practice affects you throughout the day.

Growing Spiritually:
Approaches to Prayer

Day 20

Scripture Reading: Philippians 4:6-7

Do not be anxious about anything, but in every situation, by prayer and petition, with thanksgiving, present your requests to God. And the peace of God, which transcends all understanding, will guard your hearts and your minds in Christ Jesus.

Insight

Did you choose a breath prayer yesterday? At first, praying in this way can feel forced or artificial. It can also be easy to forget during times when it could be beneficial, such as when you are stuck in traffic, or facing a tough work situation. Don't give up. The British Christian C. S. Lewis once wrote that what God wants most as we grow spiritually is that we get up and try again after every failure. If the will to walk is present, he said, God is pleased even with our stumbles.

There are many different kinds of prayer. As you develop your conversation with God, the breath prayer is only one of many approaches. Let's examine some other types of prayer that many Christians find helpful.

- Praying the Scriptures

    Praying the Scriptures connects Bible reading and prayer. You simply read a Bible verse or passage (e.g. Psalm 23:1, *"The LORD is my shepherd"*), and offer a short prayer making the verse personal (e.g.. "Lord, please be my shepherd today. Watch over and guide me"). Some people find it helpful to write their prayers. Since most of the psalms are prayers, the book of Psalms, found in the Old Testament, is a rich resource for praying the Scriptures. However, you can pray any passage in the Bible that speaks to you. Here's an example Church of the Resurrection Pastor Laurie Barnes composed, using Psalm 51:1-2:

"Have mercy on me, O God, according to your unfailing love; according to your great compassion blot out my transgressions." (Oh God, thank you for your love and forgiveness for me even when I make big mistakes.)

"Wash away all my iniquity and cleanse me from my sin." (I have trouble, Lord, trying to be all you want me to be. Thank you for wiping my slate clean and giving me the opportunity to start anew every time I confess to you.)

- Collects

The collect is a simple prayer outline Christians have used for centuries. Begin with an address to God (e.g. "Dear God"), and then acknowledge one of God's attributes (e.g. "who loves all of us"). State simply what you are praying for, using the words "so that" to say why you want it (e.g. "Please guide me so that. . ."). Then close your prayer. (By the way, *Amen*, the most common way to close a prayer, comes from a Hebrew word that means "so be it." Now you know!) Here is an example of a collect from the *Book of Common Prayer*: *Almighty God, to whom all hearts be open, all desires known, and from whom no secrets are hid; Cleanse the thoughts of our hearts by the inspiration of thy Holy Spirit, that we may perfectly love thee, and worthily magnify thy holy Name; through Christ our Lord. Amen.*

- The Poetry of Prayer

If you love beautiful language, exquisite prayers from Christians in the past can greatly bless you. Some are short but lovely. The German monk Thomas à Kempis left this gem: "As thou wilt; what thou wilt; when thou wilt." John Wesley, the British founder of Methodism, composed the longer "Covenant Prayer," which speaks eloquently of what it means to surrender our lives to Christ:

I am no longer my own, but thine.
Put me to what thou wilt, rank me with whom thou wilt.

Put me to doing, put me to suffering.
Let me be employed by thee or laid aside for thee,
exalted for thee or brought low by thee.
Let me be full, let me be empty.
Let me have all things, let me have nothing.
I freely and heartily yield all things to thy pleasure and disposal.
And now, O glorious and blessed God, Father, Son and Holy Spirit,
Thou art mine and I am thine.
So be it.
And the covenant which I have made on earth,
Let it be ratified in heaven. Amen.

Frank Laubach, a Pennsylvanian who greatly expanded literacy in the Philippines during the 20th century, often prayed: "God, what are you doing in the world today that I can help you with?" He thought that too often we ask God to bless our plans, when we might better seek to align ourselves with God's plans.

- Nonverbal prayer

    You can pray without using words. A walk through the woods or a meadow filled with wildflowers may fill your heart with praise and gratitude that reach far beyond words. For some Christians, other expressions such as dance, painting, or music become deep ways of praying. In Romans 8:26, the apostle Paul wrote that *"We do not know what we ought to pray for, but the Spirit himself intercedes for us through wordless groans."* So, however you express it, know that God "gets" your prayer.

Most Christians know the importance of prayer, but too often we find that it simply gets squeezed out of our day. We must prioritize prayer in our schedules. One suggestion is to schedule time for prayer on your day planner or calendar until it because a normal part of your daily activity and relationship with God.

Reflection Questions
1. Which of the types of prayer mentioned above do you find the most

appealing or interesting? Are there other kinds of prayer you have experienced that you found to be a blessing?

Praying the scripture + Collects.

2. Reflect on the promise of Romans 8 that the Holy Spirit intercedes for you as you pray. How does it deepen and expand your understanding of prayer to know that God helps you pray, and understands even prayers for which you do not have words?

3. Don't limit the idea of written prayers to images of dusty medieval monasteries, or your grandmother's quaint handwritten journals. How could you use the evolving forms of communication to pray? How about a Facebook prayer group? Could you text or Twitter prayers to yourself or others? Ask God to spark your creativity.

Action Step

Write four prayers, one of each type: praise, thanksgiving, confession, and asking. Make them as simple or as elaborate as you wish. Write them in this book or in another way that works for you.

Praise: Lord, you are _____

_____

Thanksgiving: God, thank you for _____

_____

Confession: Lord, I am sorry _____

_____

Asking: O God, please _____

Growing Spiritually:
Growing Spiritually Together

Scripture Reading: Colossians 3:12-17

Therefore, as God's chosen people, holy and dearly loved, clothe yourselves with compassion, kindness, humility, gentleness and patience. Bear with each other and forgive one another if any of you has a grievance against someone. Forgive as the Lord forgave you. And over all these virtues put on love, which binds them all together in perfect unity.

Let the peace of Christ rule in your hearts, since as members of one body you were called to peace. And be thankful. Let the message of Christ dwell among you richly as you teach and admonish one another with all wisdom through psalms, hymns and songs from the Spirit, singing to God with gratitude in your hearts. And whatever you do, whether in word or deed, do it all in the name of the Lord Jesus, giving thanks to God the Father through him.

Insight

Make a plan to study the Bible regularly? Check. Begin praying more frequently, in different ways and about whatever is important? Check.

That's everything we need for an exciting journey of spiritual growth, right? Almost—but not quite. You're going to need one more important thing to make this journey successfully, and that's people. Companions. A group of others with whom to travel.

Look again at today's Bible reading. Let's walk through it together.

"Clothe yourselves with compassion, kindness, humility, gentleness and patience." It's nearly impossible to exercise any of those qualities without other people to exercise them toward. Yes, you can be (and need to be)

71

gentle and patient with yourself. But you will learn more about those qualities, and understand them better, when you are also extending them to others.

"Bear with each other and forgive one another." The New Testament is full of passages that use language like this. These "one anothers" are clear evidence that the Bible writers knew that God's people would make the journey of spiritual growth together, not alone.

"Let the peace of Christ rule in your hearts, since as members of one body you were called to peace." As we discovered on Day 3, we are all members of one body—the body of Christ. Jesus connects us to one another. We belong together.

"As you teach and admonish one another." We do not make this journey passively, listening to the pastor in church once a week and otherwise keeping to ourselves. Our ability to teach and admonish one another is one of the vital elements of our spiritual growth. We do this together—we help one another.

So often today we think the word *church* means a big building, a place. We speak of "going to church," or of "the church" being at a certain address. But it was not so when the church began. Day 2 taught us that the most common word used in the New Testament for *church* was the Greek word *ekklesia*, which meant an assembly, a group of people. Even our English word *church* seems to trace back linguistically to the Greek work *kuriakos*, which meant "belonging to the Lord" and denoted the spiritual quality of the people in the church, rather than a building or a place. In the time when the New Testament was written, pretty much all of the churches were what we call "house churches"—small groups of believers who met together in someone's home to share the word of God, pray together, and encourage and support one another.

As you focus on growing spiritually, it is important that you find the "one anothers" who will be your companions on the journey. Some of the activities related to spiritual growth are things we can do in large groups of people. Worship, for instance, often seems stronger rather than weaker if we are part of a gathering of fifty, hundreds, or thousands of people. But other parts of spiritual growth, such as admonishing and teaching one another, need smaller groups more like the house churches of Bible times, where you can know one another well and provide the kind of honesty, trust, spiritual accountability, and caring that we all need to succeed on this journey.

The gospel of John says that, on the night before his crucifixion, Jesus said to his disciples, "*A new command I give you: Love one another. As I have loved you, so you must love one another. By this everyone will know that you are my disciples, if you love one another*" (John 13:34-35). The "one anothers" started with Jesus, who called us to make this journey together. They continue every day, as Christians connect with one another, encourage and teach one another, support one another, trust one another, hold one another accountable, pray for one another, and love one another. Never try to make this journey alone. Be intentional about forming the kinds of relationships that will fill your journey of spiritual growth with "one anothers."

Reflection Questions

1. Do you have anyone in your life to whom you can speak honestly about a personal spiritual struggle? If so, thank God for this relationship. If not, make it a priority to begin seeking and cultivating such friendships.

   not really.

2. Becoming a Christian does not wipe out our human quirks and problems. Reflect on our scripture passage's call to "bear with each other" and "forgive one another." How does this shape your expectations about what will happen in the relationships you form in your church? What can make practicing patience and forgiveness harder in church settings than it might be outside of the church?

3. Read Romans 12:9-21. Make a list of the qualities you want to show as you relate with others in your new church family. Put a check mark by the three you find most difficult, and regularly ask God to help you develop those qualities.

Action Step

Do you know the ways in which the church you joined helps people connect with one another? If not, ask. If necessary, ask more than once. When you find out, make a good-faith effort to take part. Do not become discouraged if you do not immediately find close, trustworthy friends (see question 2 above). It is true, of course, that sometimes the best friendships happen spontaneously, so remain open to that. But do not wait passively for that to happen—give your church's approach a chance to work for you.

Growing Spiritually:
Expect the Unexpected in Your Spiritual Growth

Scripture Reading: Ephesians 3:14-21

For this reason I kneel before the Father, from whom every family in heaven and on earth derives its name. I pray that out of his glorious riches he may strengthen you with power through his Spirit in your inner being, so that Christ may dwell in your hearts through faith. And I pray that you, being rooted and established in love, may have power, together with all the Lord's people, to grasp how wide and long and high and deep is the love of Christ, and to know this love that surpasses knowledge—that you may be filled to the measure of all the fullness of God.

Now to him who is able to do immeasurably more than all we ask or imagine, according to his power that is at work within us, to him be glory in the church and in Christ Jesus throughout all generations, for ever and ever! Amen.

Insight

We started this week of devotions by talking about Ebenezer Scrooge. In the story, everyone had given up on ol' Ebenezer. "He'll never change," they said. "His heart is as hard as stone. We'd be fools to expect any change in Ebenezer Scrooge!"

Even more, Scrooge had given up on himself. He was angry. He was bitter. He had been hurt by people, and he had determined that he would hurt people right back. Change? Him? "Bah, humbug!"

But he changed anyway. People were amazed by how he changed. He was amazed and delighted by how he changed. The wicked, miserable miser turned out to be generous. The lonely, bitter recluse had friends and family. The inhuman taskmaster discovered how to be truly human. Instead of being darkened and blighted, the lives of those around him were brightened and enriched by his presence.

A Christmas Carol is, of course, fiction. But the story it tells is true. It is the story of how, against all the odds, light overcomes darkness, good overcomes evil, and life overcomes death. It is a story buried deep in our hearts, an instinct that pops up all over the globe, in a thousand different cultures and variations.

Christians believe this is the case because the God who made us planted this story in us. This is the story God lived out in Jesus Christ. It is the story the gospel of John outlines for us: *"In the beginning was the Word, and the Word was with God, and the Word was God. . . .In him was life, and that life was the light of all people. The light shines in the darkness, and the darkness has not overcome it. . . .The true light that gives light to everyone was coming into the world. He was in the world, and though the world was made through him, the world did not recognize him. He came to that which was his own, but his own did not receive him. Yet to all who did receive him, to those who believed in his name, he gave the right to become children of God—children born not of natural descent, nor of human decision or a husband's will, but born of God"* (John 1:1, 4-5, 9-13). This story is as beautiful, sweet, and moving as any fairy tale. But there is one critical, life-giving difference: this story really happened.

And now you are a part of the story. You've joined the company of those past and present who trust that no matter where you've been and what you've done, God loves you more than you can know or imagine. You've claimed your place in the grand procession of the forgiven, those saved by God's awesome grace. And you're learning that although God loves you just the way you are, God also loves you too much to leave you that way.

You are beginning to discover what it truly means to catch a new life, to grow spiritually. You are beginning to become a changed person. You have received God's great promise made through the prophet Ezekiel: *"I will sprinkle clean water on you, and you will be clean; I will cleanse you from all your impurities and from all your idols. I will give you a new heart and put a new spirit in you; I will remove from you your heart of stone and give you a heart of flesh. And I will put my Spirit in you and move you to follow my decrees and be careful to keep my laws"* (Ezekiel 36:25-27). You are now one of the people for whom the apostle Paul prayed in today's Bible reading. You are beginning to *"be filled to the measure of all the fullness of God."* This is a life-long journey, but you have taken the first steps.

Maybe an old school friend or a family member is telling you, "You'll never change." Maybe, deep inside, you are afraid they are right. If so, hold onto the words in today's Bible passage that say God *"is able to do immeasurably more than all we ask or imagine, according to his power that is at work within us."* So expect what might be unexpected! You are on your way. You will change, and for the better. You have God's word on that!

Reflection Questions

1. When John wrote that *"the darkness has not overcome"* the light, the Roman Empire, the mightiest empire ever seen to that time, was determined to stamp out Christianity. Consider the many mighty powers since then that have tried to put out the light. Why do you believe the light always triumphs over the darkness?

2. Are there ways in which you have already sensed that God is strengthening you with power through the Holy Spirit in your inner being? In what ways are you opening yourself to the working of God's power in you?

3. What one thing that you learned or experienced this week has most strengthened and encouraged you in your journey of spiritual growth?

Action Step

Revisit the piece of paper you created at the start of the week—the one with the two columns. Pray and ask God to speak to your mind as you do this exercise. Review the first column, called "My Life Before Christ." Reflect on the qualities and actions listed that you have already left behind, or that you believe God is calling you to leave behind, and revise the list in the light of this week's learnings. Review the second column, called "My New Life in Christ." Again, reflect on the list of positive qualities and actions that you anticipate working with God to make real in your life as you journey forward in spiritual growth, and make any changes or additions this week has brought you. Place the list where you will see it often (in your Bible, on your mirror), and continue to pray over it and to review it as God leads you forward in spiritual growth.

Serving:
Not to Be Served, but to Serve

Scripture Reading: Mark 10:42-45

Jesus called them together and said, "You know that those who are regarded as rulers of the Gentiles lord it over them, and their high officials exercise authority over them. Not so with you. Instead, whoever wants to become great among you must be your servant, and whoever wants to be first must be slave of all. For even the Son of Man did not come to be served, but to serve, and to give his life as a ransom for many."

Insight

Imagine that the biggest celebrity you can think of (e.g. your favorite film star or sports hero, or the candidate you voted for in the last presidential election) has announced that he or she is going to visit your town, and you are in charge of all the arrangements! This will not be an in-and-out, 90-minute visit, either; you need to plan for a stay of several weeks, perhaps months. You're probably thinking about the best restaurants, the most comfortable lodging, a schedule that includes meetings with all of the leading citizens, and luxurious transportation because you are quite sure that is what your guest will expect. If someone said, "I'll lend you my pup tent and camp stove, and we can set things up in the vacant lot next to the laundromat," you would no doubt turn down that offer without a second thought!

Consider how things went when God, the creator and ruler of the universe, came to earth as a human being, a Galilean named Jesus. You may be familiar with some or most of the story. Jesus was born in a stable and slept in an animal feeding trough filled with straw. He grew up in a backwater town named Nazareth, a place with a bad reputation. Though he was a compelling speaker who drew large crowds, he never showed any interest in profiting financially. In fact, he once said of himself, "Foxes have holes and birds have nests, but the Son of Man has no place to lay his head" (Luke 9:58). He chose uneducated working people as his closest associates, rather than reaching out to those who could have opened doors for him through their connections. One of his followers betrayed him, and the authorities who led the Roman occupation force in Palestine executed him. He still had nothing of his own and was buried in a borrowed tomb. Christians are convinced he rose from this tomb on the third day, and the rest is history.

Jesus said he did not come to be served, but to serve. The story of his life bears that out. He used his powers in quiet acts of blessing and restoration. He directed his teaching to anyone who would listen. He showed a special affinity for the poor and the powerless, those who needed him far more than he needed them. An early Christian hymn quoted by the apostle Paul in his letter to the Philippians honored this reality, asking followers of Jesus to "have the same attitude of mind Christ Jesus had:

Who, being in very nature God,
did not consider equality with God something to be used to his own advantage;
rather, he made himself nothing
by taking the very nature of a servant,
being made in human likeness.
And being found in appearance as a human being,
he humbled himself
by becoming obedient to death—
even death on a cross!
Therefore God exalted him to the highest place
and gave him the name that is above every name,
that at the name of Jesus every knee should bow,
in heaven and on earth and under the earth,
and every tongue acknowledge that Jesus Christ is Lord,
to the glory of God the Father" (Philippians 2:5-11).

Did you catch how Paul introduced that hymn? *"Have the same attitude of mind Christ Jesus had."* When we follow Jesus, we are called to be servants, just as he was. Christianity has never been a "What's in it for me?" kind of faith. Not all of Jesus' followers through the centuries have lived in poverty; not all have been obscure and unknown. But all of Jesus' true followers share this central characteristic: they all have a servant's heart. Their primary question is, "How can I serve and bless others?" rather than, "How can I get others to serve and bless me?"

As we continue on our journey to catch a new life, we are going to learn how God equips each of us to serve, and how that shapes the way we live as God's followers. Whatever your station in life, whatever position you hold, you are called to the highest position and the greatest honor God can bestow. You are called to be a servant.

Reflection Questions

1. How does the way Jesus defined greatness in today's Bible reading compare with other definitions you have heard? In what ways do you think his concept of true greatness shaped the impact Jesus has had on the world?

2. Obviously, none of us fully understands what it is like to be God. What are some of the sacrifices you think might have been involved in Jesus choosing to live as a human being? Thank him for making those sacrifices to serve and to save all of us.

3. How did the family you grew up in view the idea of being a servant? Based on the models that helped shape you, is it somewhat natural for you to think of yourself as being a servant to others, or is it more of a struggle?

Action Step

List two or three actions that come to your mind when you hear the word *service*. Then think and pray about your inner reactions as you consider those actions. Are they things you would like to do? Things you have done, or are currently involved in? Are they things you would hope to avoid, if possible? As we go through this week's readings, see what possibilities come to mind for ways of serving that you would find joy in, and make note of them.

Serving:
The "Body of Christ"

Now to each one the manifestation of the Spirit is given for the common good. . .

Just as a body, though one, has many parts, but all its many parts form one body, so it is with Christ. For we were all baptized by one Spirit so as to form one body—whether Jews or Gentiles, slave or free—and we were all given the one Spirit to drink. Even so the body is not made up of one part but of many.

Now if the foot should say, "Because I am not a hand, I do not belong to the body," it would not for that reason cease to be part of the body. And if the ear should say, "Because I am not an eye, I do not belong to the body," it would not for that reason cease to be part of the body. If the whole body were an eye, where would the sense of hearing be? If the whole body were an ear, where would the sense of smell be? But in fact God has placed the parts in the body, every one of them, just as he wanted them to be.

Insight

When we talk about God calling each one of us to be a servant, many people feel a discouraging sense of being overwhelmed. Their inner thoughts may sound similar to this: "I know! I should serve at a soup kitchen every week. I should teach little children how to read, or tell them Bible stories. I should visit lonely people in a nursing home. I should go to Africa and help people fight AIDS. I should give more to charity, lead the United Way campaign at work, take all those extra clothes and shoes out of my closet and donate them to the Goodwill store, and sign up to work with children who have special needs. I should probably even buy a meal and give it to the homeless guy I see on the street corner all the time. I should volunteer in the nursery at church. I should sign up to serve as an usher at least once a month or begin to sing in the choir. But I don't have the time and energy to do all of those things. And I don't even want to do a lot of them! God, forgive me." Others who are less conscientious may think, "Service? I'm too busy for that."

The Bible has a message for both kinds of people, and all of us who fall somewhere in between. We can summarize that message like this: God has equipped every one of us to serve, therefore no one can say, "I have no gifts." But God has equipped us each to serve in specific ways, not to do everything in general. Because each of us is unique, you can serve in certain ways and places that no one else can fill quite as well as you can. Nothing else you do in life will bring you the joy and satisfaction that comes from finding that special, personal kind of service that fits you.

In the New Testament, the apostle Paul found a vivid way to communicate this concept of each person's uniqueness. He called the church "the body of Christ," as we have previously discussed, and compared it to our human bodies. The body is made up of many parts, and even parts that seem similar make their own unique contribution. For example, most of us have two eyes. You may think of your eyes as identical, but in fact each one makes a unique contribution to your sight, as you will discover if you ever try to play Ping-Pong with one eye covered. Depth perception depends on each eye providing a unique perspective.

In this way, each one of us is equipped to function not as the whole "body of Christ," but as one member of the body, with a distinct contribution to make. An ear may not be capable of swinging a hammer but will have a wonderful capacity for listening. The fine points of art will completely escape a foot, whose ability to carry burdens and provide balance are essential to the success of the entire body.

Paul adds that each of us has particular abilities and capacities "for the common good." In the young church at Corinth to whom this letter was addressed, it appears the members had begun to fight with one another. Some were discounting the importance of others' gifts while magnifying their own. This is why Paul imagines the absurd situation of a foot envying the hands and trying to "secede" from the body because it does not get to do what they do. Until we understand the crucial part our unique contribution plays in the overall well-being of the body, we may get caught up in envying the gifts of others.

Think of it this way: although your face almost always gets noticed more than your small intestine, it is not therefore more important to your body's health and well-being. In a similar way, Paul says, what you need is to discover which part of the body God has equipped you to be, and then serve in that unique way. Tomorrow, we will talk about how you can find your special giftedness.

Reflection Questions

1. To what extent have you tended to feel "the weight of the world" on your shoulders? How do you respond to the idea that you are one of many members of the body of Christ, called to do your part but not to carry the whole load?

2. To what extent have you tended to feel that although other people are gifted you have nothing to offer in service? How do you respond to the notion that you are uniquely equipped for a specific kind of service, and that no one else can fill that spot quite as well as you?

3. Paul says that all spiritual gifts are given "for the common good." Make an honest assessment of how much of your energy and ambition is focused on your own glory and well-being. Ask God to begin showing you how that can be redirected into activities that are focused on the common good.

Action Step

Carefully read Ephesians 4:1-16, another passage in which the idea of the body of Christ is explained. Note any new ideas the passage triggers for you, and any ways in which it helps you better understand today's reading. Spend time in prayer, asking God to help you know how these passages apply to your life.

Serving:
How to Discover Your Spiritual Gifts

Scripture Reading: 1 Corinthians 12:1, 4-6

Now about the gifts of the Spirit, brothers and sisters, I do not want you to be uninformed...

There are different kinds of gifts, but the same Spirit distributes them. There are different kinds of service, but the same Lord. There are different kinds of working, but in all of them and in everyone it is the same God at work.

Insight

Remember how exciting Christmas was when you were a kid? There were so many mysterious packages, or maybe that one big one with a funny shape you could not figure out. It seems as though most families have a special time to open packages and finally see what is inside.

Maybe you are feeling at least a little bit of that same anticipation as we approach today's subject—I hope so. It is a powerful, exciting thing to understand more clearly how you are made, what things contribute to your uniqueness, and where God has equipped you to serve. For some people, this discovery is literally life-changing!

Discovering your spiritual gifts is a three-step process:

1. Explore—First, you learn what the Bible teaches about your uniqueness, and how your spiritual gifts shape that uniqueness for service to God and others. This book offers you a quick introduction, but you will want to dig deeper. Your church may offer ways for you to explore your giftedness—if so, be sure to participate in those offerings. An excellent resource is Serving from the Heart, by Carol Cartmill and Yvonne

Gentille. The book gives you tools to help you better understand your own gifts and style, and to begin thinking about how to apply your learnings. Other excellent books, such as What You Do Best in the Body of Christ, by Bruce Bugbee, or C. Peter Wagner's Your Spiritual Gifts Can Help Your Church Grow can guide your exploration. Whatever books or classes you choose, the purpose is to understand some of the main possibilities and get a sense of which ones are the most likely to be a good fit for who you are.

2. Experience—You cannot discover with certainty that you have a spiritual gift simply by reading a book or taking a class. Once you have identified one or more gifts you think you may have, you must test that by "getting your hands dirty," seeking to use that gift or gifts to bless other people and honor God. As you are involved in concrete action, watch for two things in particular that will help you determine whether you are, in fact, using your giftedness. First, watch for effectiveness. If you are using one of your gifts, the gift should "work." If you are trying to teach, people should be learning. If you are trying to show mercy, people should be comforted and blessed. This does not mean you will immediately be as good as you can possibly get—even when we are using our gifts, we can learn and improve with experience. But you should find that you are effective. Second, watch for an inner sense of joy and rightness. Let's be clear: using your gifts will often stretch you and may take you far beyond your comfort zone. Service will not always be easy, and you will not always be "happy" in doing it. But if you are moving in the right direction, you will experience a deep sense that "this is what I was made for." And the joy that comes from that can be profound indeed.

3. Be Encouraged—if you are using your gifts, watch for and expect that other members of the body of Christ will encourage and affirm you. Be alert to this, because it is one of the ways the Holy Spirit guides you through your fellowship with other Christians. A wise approach is the "Olympic judging" approach: discard the highest score and the lowest score, and take the average of the rest. Do not put too much stock in one person who applauds what you do, but even more, do not let that one person you just can't seem to please discourage you. Let the overall

response of other members of the body help encourage you that you are on the right track, or suggest that you may need to look at adjusting your direction.

Take this process seriously, spend time in prayer, and you will discover your gifts.

Reflection Questions

1. God is at work through many different kinds of serving. List some of the various ways in which other people have blessed you. Does your list help you begin to sense the richness and variety of the ways God works?

2. Think back over your life. What are some of the high points, or times when you felt the most "alive"? Regardless of whether these high points involved some sort of "religious" activity, what clues do they give you about your giftedness?

3. What experiences of serving have you had? Think about which of them gave you some sense of "rightness." Were there any that, although you knew they were a good thing to do, left you drained of energy and joy? Again, take seriously these clues to the specific kinds of things you are gifted to do in service.

Action Step

Find out what process your church has to help you learn more about your giftedness and to connect you to satisfying, rewarding kinds of service. Take the first steps to get involved in that process. If your church does not currently offer a class, initiate a book study by inviting others to gather and study one of the books recommended above.

Serving:

Your Giftedness and God's Will

Scripture Reading: Romans 12:1-8

Therefore, I urge you, brothers and sisters, in view of God's mercy, to offer your bodies as a living sacrifice, holy and pleasing to God—this is true worship. Do not conform to the pattern of this world, but be transformed by the renewing of your mind. Then you will be able to test and approve what God's will is—his good, pleasing and perfect will.

For by the grace given me I say to every one of you: Do not think of yourself more highly than you ought, but rather think of yourself with sober judgment, in accordance with the faith God has distributed to each of you. For just as each of us has one body with many members, and these members do not all have the same function, so in Christ we, though many, form one body, and each member belongs to all the others. We have different gifts, according to the grace given to each of us. If your gift is prophesying, then prophesy in accordance with your faith; if it is serving, then serve; if it is teaching, then teach; if it is to encourage, then give encouragement; if it is giving, then give generously; if it is to lead, do it diligently; if it is to show mercy, do it cheerfully.

Insight

There are typically two types of courses in school. There are the core courses, which are the things all students are expected to learn. These classes are required, and students cannot graduate without taking them. Then there are the electives, or the subjects that only some students may have an interest in exploring. Badminton, basket-weaving, or barn architecture in the American Midwest are offered for students who want to take them; but a student can fulfill all the requirements for graduation without having badminton on his or her transcript.

Many Christians have considered learning about their giftedness for service as a kind of church "elective." They may believe the subject to be interesting or fun but do not believe it matters whether they "take the class." In today's Bible passage, we see that the apostle Paul considered it much more important than that. He viewed understanding giftedness as a "core course," with the clear-cut reason that understanding your giftedness is a key way to understand God's will for your life.

Paul begins with a stirring call to serve God, "Offer your bodies as a living sacrifice, holy and pleasing to God." He describes this as true worship, which communicates clearly that worship is not just something we do once a week in a church building. He calls us to be transformed and says that by surrendering to God in this way, we "will be able to test and approve what God's will is—his good, pleasing and perfect will." I want to know God's will. Don't you? Of course you do.

But that is a lofty goal. How do I offer myself as a living sacrifice, doing God's will for me each day? As though to directly answer that question, Paul says, "Do not think of yourself more highly than you ought, but rather think of yourself with sober judgment, in accordance with the faith God has distributed to each of you." To understand and live into God's will for us, he says, we need to think of ourselves accurately. We should not think too highly of ourselves, as though the whole weight of the world rested on us. Neither should we think of ourselves as people with nothing to offer. Instead, we need "sober judgment" about our place and our contribution.

To get that, we need to understand how God has gifted us to serve. Paul writes to the Romans a similar explanation to what he wrote to the Corinthians, "Just as each of us has one body with many members, and these members do not all have the same function, so in Christ we, though many, form one body, and each member belongs to all the others. We have different gifts, according to the grace given to each of us." And then he offers a sequence of examples: "If your gift is teaching, then teach," and so on. In other words, if, after a sober self-assessment, you are confident God has given you a certain set of gifts for service, then you can be sure God's will for your life is that you use those gifts.

Suppose a friend who has recently moved into a newly built home is planning to host an open house and asks you for help, stating, "The driveway needs to be swept, the windows need washing, and some loose boards need to be nailed down." You agree to help. When you arrive, your friend is swamped. Because you know each other well, he does not initiate conversation but rather simply hands you a broom and says, "Thanks." You're not going to stand there wondering what to do, wishing your friend could have verbally communicated his wishes, are you? And you're not going to waste time and energy trying to wash windows with a broom! You're going to go sweep the driveway because of the equipment your friend handed you.

Romans 12 says one of the best ways to know God's will for your life is to look at the equipment God has handed you! Think about yourself and your gifts with sober judgment, and you will have a good idea of where and how God wants you to serve. Then, deploy those gifts. Don't wait for the church to "tell you what to do." Look for opportunities that match up with your passions and skills, and start serving.

Reflection Questions
1. In biblical times, an animal offered as a sacrifice was, by definition, dead. What do you think Paul means when he tells us to offer ourselves as a "living" sacrifice? How does that idea help shape our approach to life?

2. Which do you find more difficult: avoiding thinking of yourself more highly than you ought, or avoiding thinking of yourself as though you have little or nothing to offer? How can you build a more accurate self-assessment?

3. Are there any ways in which your plans and wishes for yourself have changed since you gave your heart to Christ? How important is it to you that in all your choices you are following God's will rather than your own?

Action Step

Plan time for a personal retreat (a half-day at a quiet place near your home will work fine for this). Spend the time in prayer, asking God to help you think of yourself with sober judgment. Take with you a journal or some other place to record notes, so that you can write down any insights or ideas that come to you during this time. After your retreat time, talk about what you learned with two or three trusted Christian friends. Add their insights to your own learning from your retreat time.

Serving:
It's Not Just for Church

Scripture Reading: 1 Peter 4:9-11

Offer hospitality to one another without grumbling. Each of you should use whatever gift you have received to serve others, as faithful stewards of God's grace in its various forms. If you speak, you should do so as one who speaks the very words of God. If you serve, you should do so with the strength God provides, so that in all things God may be praised through Jesus Christ. To him be the glory and the power for ever and ever. Amen.

Insight

Just this morning, I spoke about service with a woman who volunteers with Pets for Life. She has a trained dog that she takes to visit older residents living in care facilities, to brighten the day for children in childcare while their parents learn English as a second language, and to many other settings where the dog is a blessing. It sounded to me like a great way to serve. Clearly she is energized and passionate about this type of service. Then she apologetically stated, "Of course, I don't do this through the church," and looked as though she expected me to declare that her volunteering in this way does not count.

She is not alone. Many times we seem to think that the only setting in which we can truly serve God is the church. Serving others through church ministries is a wonderful thing. But in today's Bible reading, you will notice that Peter said one of the reasons we serve is "so that in all things God may be praised through Jesus Christ." Not just "in all church things," but "in all things." Let's think about some of the important areas besides church where we can live out our life calling to be servants.

94

- The Marketplace

  In several places, the New Testament calls on even slaves to do their duties in a spirit of service, seeking to be a blessing to their masters (Ephesians 6:5-8; Colossians 3:22-25; Titus 2:9-10; 1 Peter 2:18-21). These verses do not show that God approves of slavery. The short letter called Philemon, in which Paul appeals to a Christian slave owner to receive a runaway slave as a "brother" rather than as a slave, makes plain that God does not approve. But calling even those who were slaves under the unfair Roman system of law to work with a spirit of service certainly tells us that all of our work and business activities are spheres in which the call to service is important.

  The marketplace opens opportunities for service that would never come our way within the confines of the church and its ministries. People who would never take anything the church does seriously will cross your path in the course of daily business. Whether you relate to them as employer or as employee, as customer or as service provider, you may be the only person God can use to touch their life. Carrying yourself always with a spirit of love and service, in all of your dealings, is a vitally important way to serve. Being ethical and honest, and going the extra mile to bless and serve, might change someone else's life eternally.

- The Home

  Many of the verses mentioned above also call Christians to bring a servant's heart to home and family relationships. Unlike many in the marketplace, these tend to be long-term relationships, which magnifies their potential for blessing and serving but also their potential for pain and hurt. It can be incredibly difficult to maintain a servant's spirit toward a parent who has treated us badly, toward a rebellious, uncooperative child, or toward a spouse with a hurtful addiction that continually interrupts our life. Service does not mean codependency—God does not want us to be doormats. But both in homes filled with light and love, and in those where challenges and pain intrude, we are called to act in the best interests of those with whom we are in relationships. Whether that means a call to take out the garbage and help with the dishes, or to deeper, more serious ways of caring, our servant calling does not end when the doors of home close behind us.

• The Community

"Love your neighbor as yourself," said the Old Testament law Jesus quoted (Leviticus 19:18). When one of his opponents asked Jesus to define who his neighbor was, Jesus responded with the story of the Good Samaritan, one of his best-loved, most far-reaching parables (Luke 10:25-37). We can bless our neighbors in so many ways, from mowing an older neighbor's lawn to organizing a Neighborhood Watch or community recycling drive.

Serving is not just for church, but for all of life. You can help make it true that "in all things God may be praised."

Reflection Questions

1. When have you been blessed by a spirit of service someone showed in the marketplace? In the home? In the community? How did those instances affect you?

2. Do you believe that being ethical and honest, and "going the extra mile" by helping in ways that you are not required to, is good business or bad business? When you are treated that way, how does it affect your feelings as a customer? How could it potentially affect someone's life eternally?

3. In today's reading, Peter says that we are to be faithful stewards of whatever gifts we have received. What does it mean to you to be a steward? (If you are not sure, look up the word's meaning.) How, if at all, have this week's readings changed your attitude about your gifts?

Action Step

List people and situations in which you have opportunities to be a servant in the marketplace, in your home, and in your community. Outline specific plans to more fully live out a spirit of service in each of those settings.

Serving:
Sharing the Good News through Your Gifts

Scripture Reading: 1 Peter 3:15-16

But in your hearts revere Christ as Lord. Always be prepared to give an answer to everyone who asks you to give the reason for the hope that you have. But do this with gentleness and respect, keeping a clear conscience, so that those who speak maliciously against your good behavior in Christ may be ashamed of their slander.

Insight

Who told you about Jesus? Who influenced you to decide to follow him? It may have been one person, or it may have been many different people, playing different parts at different times in your life. It may have been a preacher addressing a large audience, or it may have been a friend sitting with you over coffee.

However it happened for you, hearing about Jesus is an activity that has gone for over 2000 years. The New Testament has a word for one person telling another about Jesus—*euangelizō*, which is a Greek word meaning "to share good news." That was a good fit. What better news could there be to share than Jesus' love, grace, and victory over death? The Greek word may feel somewhat familiar to you, as the English words *evangelize* and *evangelist* stem from its Greek root.

Unfortunately, the word *evangelist* can sometimes conjure images of a charismatic but unscrupulous Elmer Gantry-like character. Some even forget that the word ever existed without the prefix *tele* attached to it! But, biblically, evangelizing means one person sharing the good news of Jesus with someone else. This is a particularly powerful and life-changing form of service, one we can all be a part of.

What we have been learning about our unique giftedness for service helps us discern how we are a part of evangelism. Ephesians 4:11 says that Christ gave some the task of being "evangelists," from which we can discern that God gives some of us a special giftedness for sharing Christ with others, though in many different ways. British writer John Stott suggests that "it may refer to the gift of evangelistic preaching, or of making the gospel particularly plain and relevant to unbelievers, or of helping timorous people to take the plunge of commitment to Christ, or of effective personal witnessing. Probably the gift of an evangelist may take all these different forms and more" (p. 163).

For those whom God has gifted in this way, evangelism becomes one of the main ways they serve. It energizes them, engages all of their creativity and passion, and gives them profound inner satisfaction. The apostle Paul was one such gifted evangelist. Acts 14:19-20 describes how people in the city of Lystra stoned Paul and dragged him outside of the town, thinking they had killed him. But when Paul regained consciousness, he matter-of-factly traveled to the city of Derbe and continued preaching Jesus. For him, it was unimaginable that he would give up sharing the faith, even in the most hazardous conditions. That is wonderful, but we do not all have this gift.

Although we know from Ephesians that God gave "some" the spiritual gift of evangelism, that does not mean the rest of us can forget about sharing our faith. In today's reading, Peter urges all of us, not just some of us, to "*always be prepared to give an answer to everyone who asks*" about the hope we have. If you have the gift of approaching total strangers and effectively sharing the good news, by all means use it. But if you break into a cold sweat at the thought of that kind of sharing, as you use your gifts and live with a spirit of service you will still have times when someone will ask you a question that provides an opportunity for you to share your faith. "How come you have so much peace?" they may ask, or, "Do you really believe that story about Jesus' resurrection?" At those moments, Peter says, be ready to give an answer. Watch for those occasions, and ask the Holy Spirit to help you when they come. Often, God seems to use this type of sharing to reach people who are too closed or scared ever to listen to a gifted evangelist. Sometimes a quiet word of sharing from a trusted friend or co-worker is the only channel God has available.

So we all get to take part in the wonderful service of evangelizing, even though only some of us are gifted to be evangelists. Always be ready.

Reflection Questions

1. In what ways has Jesus' steadfast love and grace been good news in your life?

2. Have you known or heard anyone you would consider a gifted evangelist? Did one or more such people play a role in your decision to become a Christian? Do you think evangelism might be one of your spiritual gifts?

3. When you see a movie you enjoy, or try a new restaurant and really like the food, do you tell anyone else about it? Do you find it awkward or embarrassing to share that kind of information with friends? Think about how that may provide a model for sharing the good news of Jesus.

Action Step

Spend time writing out your answer to the following questions: 1) "Why do you believe in Jesus?" and 2) "What does following Jesus mean to you?" Get together with a Christian friend, and practice sharing your answers with one another so that you will be ready to share when opportunities arise.

Note:

Stott, John. *God's New Society: The Message of Ephesians*. Downers Grove, Ill.: InterVarsity Press, 1980.

Serving:
Expect the Unexpected as You Serve

Scripture Reading: 2 Timothy 1:6-7

For this reason I remind you to fan into flame the gift of God, which is in you through the laying on of my hands. For the Spirit God gave us does not make us timid, but gives us power, love and self-discipline.

Insight

Darrell Holtz, who contributed to the writing of this devotional, tells about knowing a man who worked all of his life as a doctor. For much of the time, this man hated his job. He looked forward to days off and could hardly wait for vacations. He retired as soon as he was able, and he promised himself that he would never make hospital calls again if he could help it. Retirement, however, did not bring him automatic happiness. He still had a lot of anger, as well as some destructive habits. With some encouragement from his wife, he decided to get involved with a church, something he had discarded years earlier. After some searching, they joined the church I belong to.

Transformation did not happen all at once, but this man began to change. He found the power to set aside his destructive habits. He found an outlet for his love of music in being a faithful choir member. He learned that God was calling him to service, and he began to explore what gifts he might have. He talked with one of the pastors about how he could help with the work of offering spiritual care and support to others in the church. The pastor told him she thought he would be good at visiting members in the hospital, and encouraging and praying with them. His immediate response was, "No! I want to help, but not that way." But the pastor did not back off. Her suggestion was not random; she honestly felt that she was discerning a special giftedness in him for that kind of service.

Finally, reluctantly, he agreed to try. He was startled to find he did not hate this particular form of service but instead found it a blessing. Additionally, he almost instantly received affirming confirmation from the members of the body of Christ that he visited. Now he makes hospital calls several times a week. And he loves it! He has a deep sense of calling about his ministry. He knows that he is using his giftedness to serve others and bring glory to God. A smile lights his face when he talks about making hospital calls. He has found the unique place of service God equipped him to fill.

I know people who have always loved the comforts of home yet now eagerly look forward to the chance to spend time in Honduras or South Africa, blessing those who live in uncomfortable conditions. I know people who used to say, "I never read a book," who now eagerly look forward to leading Bible studies and going deep into the questions that arise in their class. I know people who used to live to make money who now find great joy in giving away large amounts of their money to bless others.

A distinguished religious teacher named Nicodemus came to see Jesus. He expected to ask some textbook questions, get some textbook answers, and go home to resume his life. Instead, he found himself immediately challenged, stretched and confused by Jesus' words. Sensing his consternation, Jesus said, *"Don't be so surprised when I tell you that you have to be 'born from above'—out of this world, so to speak. You know well enough how the wind blows this way and that. You hear it rustling through the trees, but you have no idea where it comes from or where it's headed next. That's the way it is with everyone 'born from above' by the wind of God, the Spirit of God"* (John 3:7-8, *THE MESSAGE*).

You have set out to catch a new life and follow Jesus, who is calling you to be a servant, to use your gifts and your uniqueness to fill a spot no one else can fill quite like you. Is that an unexpected surprise to you? Or do you feel like you are finally settling into something you've always sensed you were meant to do? "The wind blows this way and that." Stay open to God's Spirit, and let that wind blow you in the direction God wants you to go.

Reflection Questions
1. Based on this week's readings, how important do you believe it is for you to be involved in service? How important do you believe it is for you to be involved in the kind of service God has equipped you to do?

2. What are some ways you can take your gifts and "fan them into flame"? How can you encourage others to fan their gifts into flame?

3. When have you seen the "wind" of the Holy Spirit blow through your own life, or the life of someone close to you, and produce a surprisingly wonderful outcome?

Action Step

Go back to the list you made after day 21. Add any notes you have made or thoughts that have come to you this week about ways of serving that you would find joy in. Pray over the list, asking God's Spirit to impress upon you the directions that God is calling you to explore at this point in your life. Take the next step if you have not done so already, and volunteer.

Day 30

Giving:
Understanding God as the Creator and Owner of Resources

Scripture Reading: 1 Chronicles 29:10-14

David praised the LORD in the presence of the whole assembly, saying, "Praise be to you, LORD, the God of our father Israel, from everlasting to everlasting. Yours, LORD, is the greatness and the power and the glory and the majesty and the splendor, for everything in heaven and earth is yours. Yours, LORD, is the kingdom; you are exalted as head over all. Wealth and honor come from you; you are the ruler of all things. In your hands are strength and power to exalt and give strength to all. Now, our God, we give you thanks, and praise your glorious name.

"But who am I, and who are my people, that we should be able to give as generously as this? Everything comes from you, and we have given you only what comes from your hand.

Insight

After learning to say "momma," "dada," and "no," young children seem quickly to add the following word to their expanding vocabulary: *mine*. From a very early age, we live in a mindset of "mine, mine, mine." But what is "ours," really? The Bible tells us that God created the earth and everything in the earth. *"The earth is the LORD's, and everything in it, the world, and all who live in it"* (Psalm 24:1). So if God is the creator of everything, then it follows that God is the owner of everything.

To understand God as owner of *everything* is a radical, counter-cultural concept in today's society. We work hard and have legal documents verifying that our car, our house, our bank accounts, and our identity belong to us. We put our names on the things that belong to us as a way of identifying what is ours. My grandmother used to label all of her dishes, clothing, knickknacks, and even her tape dispenser with her initials. She wanted there to be no mistake that in her living, and even in her dying, these items belonged to her.

But if everything really belongs to God, what does this mean for us? What are the implications? We begin by recognizing that God is the rightful owner of all our things. Today's scripture passage reminds us that everything in heaven and earth belongs to God, which means that all power and glory are to be given to God. We are called to be stewards of these resources. God gives us the ability, talent, and strength to work, and in our response of giving, we actually give back to God what is already God's.

As a new member, you will likely hear your pastor or other church members use the words *stewardship* and *generosity*. Often, the word stewardship brings to mind the image that all the church really wants is "my money." But stewardship and generosity are more than finances that support your local church. This is a way of life. According to the dictionary, a steward is one who "manages the property, finances or household of another." In ancient times, a steward was someone who managed the affairs of the king. As stewards of God's kingdom, we are called to be generous givers as we provide for the ministry and mission of the household of God.

Stewardardship involves the giving of your time, talents, abilities, and relationships. And yes, stewardship of the financial resources God has entrusted to you is a part of the commitment you made when joining the church. Financial generosity to the church is one expression of worship and love for God. As we reflect on God's goodness and respond to God's love, our hearts are moved to generosity. Stewardship is an act of discipleship, another way in which to put God first in your life, resulting in spiritual growth and depth.

The ministry of your church is not possible without your resources of time, prayer, and money. You support your church through your offerings. Every local church has expenses related to the operating of the building, offering excellent programming, and reaching out in mission to the community. Over the next seven days, consider more fully what God wants to do through you and what priorities may need to be realigned in your life as you seek to participate faithfully in the mission and ministry of your church. Discover what it means to bring glory and honor to God through your giving.

Reflection Questions

1. Think of a time when you cared for something that did not belong to you. How did you feel? What is your reaction to the discoveries that "everything we have belongs to God" and that we are to be stewards of the gifts God has given us?

2. What does *steward* mean? What do you see as the connection between the stewardship of your own time, talent, and financial resources and what God is able to do through your local church?

3. How does the understanding that God is the owner of everything you have reshape your thinking about your possessions and finances, and the decision you make to give financially to your church?

Action Step

Make a list of the ways you benefit from the ministries of your church. What programs do you enjoy participating in? How does your church reach out to your community in mission? Consider even obvious things, such as having the appropriate temperature in the building for worship, paper towels in the restroom, hymnals, pens, weekly worship bulletins, a parking space for your car, a Web site, etc. Each of these items has a cost, and the financial gifts of church members make the purchase and upkeep of these items possible.

Giving:
Old Testament
Understanding of the Tithe

Scripture Reading: Genesis 14:17-20

After Abram returned from defeating Kedorlaomer and the kings allied with him, the king of Sodom came out to meet him in the Valley of Shaveh (that is, the King's Valley). Then Melchizedek king of Salem brought out bread and wine. He was priest of God Most High, and he blessed Abram, saying,

"Blessed be Abram by God Most High,
Creator of heaven and earth.
And praise be to God Most High,
who delivered your enemies into your hand."
Then Abram gave him a tenth of everything.

Insight

We live in a society where we are bombarded with financial wisdom. Every major media outlet has a "money expert." We have 24-hour financial channels. Radio and TV talk show hosts provide advice on how to budget and spend our financial resources. All of these resources provide advice on how to get ahead so that we can have resources available to do the things we would like to do. And yet, some of us are barely making ends meet. We struggle to pay our bills and reduce debt. Moreover, as members of the church, we are called to "tithe," which may feel like one more "bill" or obligation to pay.

Our culture views money as a private, personal matter. Many of us struggle with the idea of giving to the church, yet God intends our gift, or tithe, to be a joy and a blessing.

The word *tithe* comes from an Old English word meaning "tenth." Tithing simply means giving back to God 10 percent of one's earnings. In the Old

Testament we read that the Israelites were required to give 10 percent of everything they earned and grew to the temple (Leviticus 27:30; Numbers 18:26).

The first account of this practice in the Bible is found in today's scripture passage. In Genesis 14:17-20, Abraham (then named Abram) had just won in battle. Scripture tells us that he tithed the spoils of his victory to Melchizedek, the priest of God Most High, as a way of giving praise and glory to God. Abraham understood tithing as an appropriate way to honor God with his physical possessions and recognized God as the one who made his victory possible.

The tithe captures the idea of putting God first, acknowledging that God alone gives us everything we have, so our tithe is a way to present a meaningful offering that expresses our gratitude. Deuteronomy 26:1-15 records the Israelites giving a tenth of their harvest as a sign of gratitude to God. The tithe was then used to support the work of the temple in caring for the needy and holding worship celebrations for the people.

Today the practice of tithing still plays a vital role in life of your church. Through members' tithes, your church is able to plan and budget for quality ministry programming, hold worship services each weekend, and provide outreach and mission to care for the poor and needy in your community. Because the tithe was established as a way to demonstrate love for God, neglecting this practice has an impact on the work God wants to do through you and your church.

Malachi 3:8-12 provides an example of how the people tried to avoid giving fully to God what was required. *"Will a mere mortal rob God? Yet you rob me. But you ask, 'How are we robbing you?' 'In tithes and offerings. You are under a curse—your whole nation—because you are robbing me. Bring the whole tithe into the storehouse, that there may be food in my house. Test me in this,' says the LORD Almighty, 'and see if I will not throw open the floodgates of heaven and pour out so much blessing that there will not be room enough to store it. I will prevent pests from devouring your crops, and the vines in your fields will not drop their fruit before it is ripe,' says the LORD Almighty. 'Then all the nations will call you blessed, for yours will be a delightful land,' says the LORD Almighty."*

Failure to tithe, the people are told in this passage, is like robbing God. God promises that renewed obedience in tithing will result in blessings so abundant *"there will not be room enough to store it all."* Through generous giving, we experience great joy.

As a member of the church, do you make God first in your life, offering your heart and praise as evidenced by your financial support of the work of the church? Or do you believe that you cannot fully support God's work with your finances for whatever reason? If so, set tithing as a goal. Make an intentional decision today to develop a plan of giving, making a commitment you can fulfill and moving toward the tithe. Think of tithing as an opportunity versus an obligation—an opportunity to express your love and gratitude for all that God has provided you. Through your gifts and offerings, others will be blessed.

Reflection Questions

1. The readings today help us understand the tithe as a guide. Do you think the tithe is still relevant today? Why or why not? How does putting God first in your finances help fulfill God's purposes for your life? Your church?

2. What feelings do you have when you think of tithing? Does it frighten you? Excite you? If you do not tithe, what do you think of the idea of making this a goal in your Christian life?

3. How do Genesis 14:17-20; Deuteronomy 26:1-15; and Malachi 3:8-12 reflect the idea of giving out of gratitude for receiving? How well does your giving to the church reflect the honor and praise you give to God?

Action Step

As you begin, take time to pray. Thank God for the resources entrusted to you. Ask God to show you areas you need to surrender. Do a quick audit of your finances. Do they reflect your love for God? What changes are needed in your life to trust the Lord with your finances?

Giving:
The Teachings of the New Testament on Giving

Scripture Reading: 2 Corinthians 9:6-15

Remember this: Whoever sows sparingly will also reap sparingly, and whoever sows generously will also reap generously. Each of you should give what you have decided in your heart to give, not reluctantly or under compulsion, for God loves a cheerful giver. And God is able to bless you abundantly, so that in all things at all times, having all that you need, you will abound in every good work. As it is written: "They have scattered abroad their gifts to the poor; their righteousness endures forever." Now he who supplies seed to the sower and bread for food will also supply and increase your store of seed and will enlarge the harvest of your righteousness. You will be made rich in every way so that you can be generous on every occasion, and through us your generosity will result in thanksgiving to God. This service that you perform is not only supplying the needs of the Lord's people but is also overflowing in many expressions of thanks to God. Because of the service by which you have proved yourselves, people will praise God for the obedience that accompanies your confession of the gospel of Christ, and for your generosity in sharing with them and with everyone else. And in their prayers for you their hearts will go out to you, because of the surpassing grace God has given you. Thanks be to God for his indescribable gift!

Insight

Many believe the church today speaks too often about money. Interestingly, in the New Testament Jesus speaks more about money, resources, and giving than about the importance of prayer. He knew our spiritual life would be challenged by money and possessions and that we would always desire more.

He knew our natural human inclination would be to acquire and accumulate things rather than to give.

From the beginning, although we had been given everything we needed, we desired more. Adam and Eve were not satisfied with the perfect garden. They wanted the one thing God told them they could not have, and they ran after it. Jesus talked about this desire to accumulate more and more. In Matthew 6:32-33, he tells us that people who do not know God "run after" material things, and he instructs us instead to *"seek first [God's] kingdom and his righteousness."*

We need transformation to become a giving people who seek God's kingdom first. And the process of transformation as we become more Christlike is ongoing.

At the beginning of our Christian walk, we may have had the idea that everything we possess is ours. We may have since moved to a realization that what we have is God's, but we may still struggle to let go totally. Through the process of transformation, we ultimately acknowledge that all we have is God's, nothing is ours, and we are the stewards and caretakers of these resources.

Although the Old Testament was specific about the tithe, the New Testament teaches why our giving is important, the spirit in which we are to give, and the benefits of giving. (In the New Testament, there is a reference to Abraham's gift of a tenth in Hebrews 7:1-10.)

In Second Corinthians, Paul writes to the members of the church in Corinth, asking them to take up a collection for those who are in need. This is actually Paul's second letter to this church. He is following up to encourage the church members to do what they had previously promised they would do.

This passage teaches the following about giving:

- There is a relationship between giving and receiving (v. 6).
- God loves a cheerful giver motivated not from duty but out of love for God (v. 7).
- God multiplies our giving to meet the needs of others (v. 8).
- Others glorify God because of the example set in our generosity (v. 13).
- God's grace at work in our lives is an indescribable gift (vv. 14-15).

As a new member, you will be invited to participate in the giving of your financial resources to benefit others who are in need and to help further the mission and ministry of God at work through your church. Many motives may prompt your giving, such as a sense of duty or habit. But the highest motivation for your decision to give is love—love for God and love for others.

Generosity is a joyful expression of your relationship with God, and your desire to make God first in your life as you seek his Kingdom and his righteousness. In your giving you will discover the connection between giving and receiving, and the indescribable gift of God's grace. Because of this grace and its transforming work in our lives, we should think not, "How little can I give?" but rather, "How much can I give?"

Reflection Questions

1. Where in society do you see the desire for "more, more, more" lived out? What about in your own life?

2. In Second Corinthians we discover we are called to be *cheerful givers*. What does that mean to you personally? Where do you struggle with being cheerful in your generosity? What should motivate your giving? How are you beginning to think about your attitude of giving?

3. Who benefits from your giving to the church?

Action Step

Take a "stewardship walk" around your church. Visit the sanctuary, children's nursery, mission collection area, etc. How do you see God using church members' giving in ministry and mission to others? What do you see as the connection between the stewardship and generosity of your financial resources and what God is able to do through your local church?

Giving:
A Formula for Giving to the Church

Scripture Reading: Mark 12:41-44

Jesus sat down opposite the place where the offerings were put and watched the crowd putting their money into the temple treasury. Many rich people threw in large amounts. But a poor widow came and put in two very small copper coins, worth only a fraction of a penny.

Calling his disciples to him, Jesus said, "Truly I tell you, this poor widow has put more into the treasury than all the others. They all gave out of their wealth; but she, out of her poverty, put in everything—all she had to live on."

Insight

At some point, your church will most likely ask you to complete a commitment card indicating an estimate of your giving. There are two reasons why this is important. The first we have touched on in previous readings. The process of making a commitment to serve God with your financial gift is an act of worship and an expression of your love and gratitude to God. Second, your commitment allows your church to budget and plan for its ministries and programs in the days ahead.

You may wonder how much you should give to the church. In the Old Testament we read the command to tithe ten percent (Genesis 14:17-20; 28:20-22; Leviticus 27:30-33; Numbers 18:26-29). The New Testament focuses more on the attitude with which we are to give (Matthew 10:8; 19:21; Luke 6:38; 12:32-34; Acts 20:35). Through willing and cheerful giving, we honor God while supporting the work of the church. Although our previous reading in Malachi 3:8-12 equates withholding tithes to robbing God, God does not force us to tithe but instead invites us to participate in God's work.

"Each of you should give what you have decided in your heart to give, not reluctantly or under compulsion, for God loves a cheerful giver" (2 Corinthians 9:7).

Scripture tells us that we should give as we are able. Sometimes that may mean giving more than ten percent, and sometimes it may mean giving less, depending upon the ability of the individual. The necessities of life currently consume much of the income of many individuals and families. Making a decision to give is a deep matter of faith. Although the tithe may be a goal, it may be something you will have to work toward as you make adjustments in your priorities. The important thing is to take a next step and offer what you are able.

While watching people bring offerings to the temple, Jesus shares with us a teachable moment. Several rich people contributed large sums of money, while a widow contributed two small coins worth only a fraction of a penny. Who gave more? It may seem obvious that those who put in more money gave more, but this passage teaches us to understand giving from a fundamentally different perspective. The wealthy gave out of their abundance, but the widow generously gave from all that she had. In proportion to her income, she gave more of herself to honor God, becoming an example and a reminder that our giving is not about comparing ourselves with other people. Giving is about making a decision of faith that makes a difference in shaping your life in Christ.

In giving back to God, you enter into a special relationship. You dedicate yourself to serve God and financially support the work of the church. In return, God promises to bless you. Giving, then, is an intensely personal matter between you and God—a way of demonstrating the depth of your commitment and relationship. It is not predicated on a mandatory formula or percentage but instead is a response that flows from your heart.

Reflection Questions

1. Why do you think Jesus was watching people give their offerings? What do you think he was looking for?

2. What example did this woman set for us? How was Jesus' heart touched

by her offering? Think of someone who has been an example of generous giving. What has that person modeled for you?

3. What are you most excited about as you consider how God might use your resources? How does this help you become a cheerful giver? How is your decision to give reshaping your life?

Action Step

The widow gave what she had because she believed God and the work of the temple were worth the sacrifice. As you consider what you will commit to the church, make a list of why you believe your giving is worth the sacrifice.

Giving:
The Discipline of Giving

Scripture Reading: Matthew 6:19-24

"Do not store up for yourselves treasures on earth, where moth and rust destroy, and where thieves break in and steal. But store up for yourselves treasures in heaven, where moth and rust do not destroy, and where thieves do not break in and steal. For where your treasure is, there your heart will be also.

"The eye is the lamp of the body. If your eyes are healthy, your whole body will be full of light. But if your eyes are unhealthy, your whole body will be full of darkness. If then the light within you is darkness, how great is that darkness!

"No one can serve two masters. Either you will hate the one and love the other, or you will be devoted to the one and despise the other. You cannot serve both God and Money."

Insights

When you were young, you might have saved important things by putting them in a shoebox or some other such safe place. You might have believed these things to be treasures, and you might have hidden that shoebox because you believed it protected them. You may not have that shoebox today, but you may still protect your treasures, the largest of which is most likely your money.

Today's passage may have challenged you to consider what it could mean to give generously to God and the work of the church. The thought of giving ten percent may make you wonder about your priorities and worry about how you will be able to make ends meet. You may fear that it means you will never be able to move to the larger house you had been saving for, purchase a newer, more reliable car, take a dream vacation, or get out of debt.

Scripture tells us that we cannot serve two masters. The key is to find a balance of how we view money and how we spend money. The verses that follow our reading for today (Matthew 6:25-34) tell us we are not to be anxious or worry about money. If we worry about money, we tend to hold on to it tightly. We are then afraid to give to the church because we worry there will not be enough left to meet our own needs. Whether we have been blessed with ample resources or we struggle each month to make ends meet, Jesus still tells us to "*seek first [God's] kingdom.*" When we do this, we find the balance that leads to true contentment.

So how do we determine what we can give? Below are a few ideas:
1. Start by developing a budget. Consider tithing first (designating a percentage from your income to give to the church), saving second, and paying for essentials next. There are several online tools. You may also want to consider taking a financial class through Financial Peace University or Crown Financial Ministries to learn how to manage more effectively the resources God has given you.
2. As you look at your budget, think about where can you reduce your spending so that you can tithe, save, and have money to give to others.
3. Before you make a purchase, consider how much you will use that purchase and whether it is a good value.
4. Surround this process in prayer. Ask, "Lord, what are you calling the church to do? As a member of the church, what will you do through me?" As you consider how much you can give, pray until you feel confident you are making the best decision in your present circumstance.
5. Respond faithfully with confidence and boldness.

Making a financial commitment to support the work of the church is an important decision. The process of making this decision requires first and foremost time spent in prayer. During prayer, we seek the same thing Jesus sought when he called out to God, "*May your will be done*" (Matthew 26:42). Prayer prepares our hearts for the transforming work of Christ in our lives and the shaping of our attitudes, and it prepares us to take bold steps of faith.

In the end, your decision to give financially to God through an offering to your church may mean giving up a few things you currently enjoy (earthly treasures) so that you can invest resources into something that you have come to love more, Jesus Christ.

Reflection Questions

1. What does it mean to serve two masters? How do you see this idea of serving both God and money played out in today's society? Where in your life are you trying to serve two masters?

2. Why does having too much or too little distract us from God? Do you worry about money? How does this worry distract you from fully discovering God's will for your life?

3. What do you think it means to seek first the kingdom of God?

Action Step

Take time this week to study your budget. How much can you give? In what areas do you need to grow in faith and trust God with your resources? Pray about this decision until you feel comfortable.

Giving:
Receiving and Giving

Scripture Reading: Matthew 10:8

Freely you have received, freely give.

Insight

In the movie *Pay It Forward* students are challenged by their teacher to find a way to change the world for the better and put their plan into action. One student has the idea of doing a favor for someone without any expectation of being paid back and encouraging that person to do something for someone else. His plan was that the desire to help another person would spread exponentially, with the goal of making the world a better place. *Pay It Forward* is the story of ordinary people doing extraordinary things for others.

The Bible is full of such stories—ordinary people doing extraordinary things to help change the world for the better. Jesus initiates this idea, stating, "*Freely you have received, freely give.*"

In this passage, we find Jesus sitting with his disciples preparing to send them out. The disciples had been with Jesus, watching the example he set as he preached the good news of the Kingdom and cared for the needs of people. He then tells them to go and do likewise. I imagine the apostles listening with great intensity at that moment, for they were just ordinary people who may not have believed they had anything to give. Jesus was telling them, however, to go out and do as he had done.

You have joined a church and are now an active member of a worshiping community. At some point in the past, ordinary people gave freely so that you would have a place to worship, a seat to sit in, and the opportunity to participate in ministry programs and Bible studies. People gave because they were motivated by their love for Christ and had the desire to give back to God what God rightfully owns. They gave generously to the church so that others might come to know Christ.

In your financial commitment to the church, you are doing the same, giving freely of your resources without expectation of receiving anything in return, motivated by love and the realization that you have received freely from the life-changing work of Christ in your life and others who have given generously to the work of your church in the past.

Each weekend when you arrive for worship and have a seat to sit in, a choir to lead music, a hymnal to follow along as you join in song, coffee in the foyer, and a place to connect with others, consider that this is possible only because of the generosity of others sitting around you in the congregation.

As a member of the church, you are now being invited into this life-giving work. Christ's love compels us with a great desire to give to others and to live generous lives by contributing to the work of the church. What happens when you decide to show love in a tangible way by the giving of your resources? What happens when you choose to live with the mindset that because you have freely received, you should therefore freely give?

Now is your time to find out what an extraordinary difference an ordinary person can make. Knowing how much God has given, let us be impassioned to give back by giving to others, expecting nothing in return.

Reflection Questions

1. What do you think the disciples were feeling when Jesus gave them instructions to go out and do what he had been modeling for them? Put yourself in this gathering, and consider what you would have felt. Would you have been anxious, fearful, overwhelmed, excited, passionate, or something else?

2. What have you freely received from God? How does knowing you have received something freely make you feel? What command are we given? How does knowing God uses ordinary people to do extraordinary things compel you to want to give more?

3. What have you received by being a part of your church community?

Action Step

Take time to reflect on your experience with giving and receiving. Have you experienced someone giving something to you with no expectation of anything in return? What do you remember? As you think about your church, make a list of those things you have received "freely" as a part of the generosity of others. Some of the items on your list may not be tangible but may instead be things like friendship, etc.

Day 36

Giving:
Expecting the Unexpected through Giving as You Encounter the Living God

Scripture Reading: Luke 9:10-17

When the apostles returned, they reported to Jesus what they had done. Then he took them with him and they withdrew by themselves to a town called Bethsaida, but the crowds learned about it and followed him. He welcomed them and spoke to them about the kingdom of God, and healed those who needed healing.

Late in the afternoon the Twelve came to him and said, "Send the crowd away so they can go to the surrounding villages and countryside and find food and lodging, because we are in a remote place here."

He replied, "You give them something to eat."

They answered, "We have only five loaves of bread and two fish—unless we go and buy food for all this crowd." (About five thousand men were there.)

But he said to his disciples, "Have them sit down in groups of about fifty each." The disciples did so, and everyone sat down. Taking the five loaves and the two fish and looking up to heaven, he gave thanks and broke them. Then he gave them to the disciples to set before the people. They all ate and were satisfied, and the disciples picked up twelve basketfuls of broken pieces that were left over.

Insight

We live in a society in which we often wonder if what we have is "enough." Do I have enough money to pay my bills? Do I have enough food to feed my family? Have I have saved enough to provide for me in retirement? Do I have enough to contribute in any significant way to the work of the church?

God does not require us to analyze whether what we have is "enough." God

122

asks us to be faithful with whatever we have available, no matter how large or how small the contribution. God takes whatever we can give and uses it in powerful, life-giving ways. The question then shifts from, "Do I have enough to give?" to, "Will I give from what I have?"

The disciples learned this lesson. Immediately following the command to go out and "freely give," they returned exhilarated and excited to share with Jesus all they had experienced. Jesus knew they were tired and suggested they go to a quiet place to rest, but word was spreading quickly about the powerful things he and the disciples were doing. People in need of healing and hope starting coming from all directions in search of them. Scripture tells us there were more than 5,000 people in the crowd on one particular occasion.

Jesus had compassion for the people and told the disciples to give them something to eat. After the disciples took inventory of what was available—two fish and five loaves of bread—they told Jesus there was not enough. They suggested that Jesus send the people away to find food somewhere else.

This is an interesting turn of events. The disciples had just been given a command to give freely, because they had freely received. And almost immediately they were not willing to give what they had available because they feared it would not be enough. They were afraid that such a small contribution would not make a big difference.

Too often, our human nature is to tell ourselves that what we have to offer is not enough to matter. We either decide to do nothing or come up with alternative ideas that do not directly involve us. We hang on to our resources. But as he did with the disciples, Jesus wants to teach us another lesson.

So far in the story, a hungry crowd of people has gathered around Jesus, and the disciples have no food for them. Determining there is no way to provide for that many people, they disciples recommend they be sent away. But Jesus does not let the disciples off the hook. "You feed them," he says. The disciples protest, declaring, "We can't. We don't have enough!" When they tell Jesus they have only five loaves and two fish, he does the unexpected, multiplying what is available in order to feed the crowd.

The disciples voluntarily gave the loaves and fish. Until they were willing to commit what they had, Jesus waited. Their contribution and commitment, though seemingly inadequate, were part of the solution. When the disciples gave from what was available, Jesus took their gift, blessed it, and told the disciples to distribute it to all the people. Scripture tells us that everyone in the crowd was fed, and there were twelve baskets of leftovers.

This story leaves us with important reminders as we consider what we will give of our resources to the work of the church:

1. God asks that we take an inventory of what we have available and offer our resources to be used for ministry and mission—preaching the good news and caring for the needs of others.
2. No matter how small our gift, we are to release control, giving cheerfully and willingly.
3. When we give, we discover the unexpected. The living God takes our gifts, blessing and multiplying them more powerfully than we could have imagined.

Giving your resources is a process, an experience that requires faith. How many loaves do you have? Go and see, and be prepared to experience the unexpected as you encounter the living God through your giving.

Reflection Questions

1. Jesus could have miraculously fed all of the people on his own. Why do you think he waited for the disciples to respond? How do you think the disciples were feeling as they took inventory of what was available?

2. What happened when the disciples turned over control of their resources to Jesus? What lesson does this story hold for you?

3. What are you learning about how God works through people? How do you see this lived out in your church?

Action Step

Request a commitment card from your stewardship committee. Prayerfully make a commitment to give of your financial resources to the work of the church.

Church Membership:
What Is It?

Scripture Reading: Ephesians 4:10-13

He handed out gifts above and below, filled heaven with his gifts, filled earth with his gifts. He handed out gifts of apostle, prophet, evangelist, and pastor-teacher to train Christ's followers in skilled servant work, working within Christ's body, the church, until we're all moving rhythmically and easily with each other, efficient and graceful in response to God's Son, fully mature adults, fully developed within and without, fully alive like Christ. (THE MESSAGE)

Insight

You have said, "I do," to Jesus to be a part of the church, the bride of Christ. Throughout our study, we have explored what it means to be the church, to grow spiritually, to serve God, and to give. But what exactly does it mean to be a member of a local church?

Membership expectations vary from denomination to denomination, and local church to local church. What we share in common is an understanding of our call to be the body of Christ. You have become a member of a community of people who profess that Jesus Christ is Lord, who gather as a faith community committed to care for one another and encourage one another to grow in grace and knowledge, and who share the good news of Jesus Christ with a hurting world.

If you have ever become a member of a country club, health center, or even a credit card program, you know membership has many privileges. When you join a church, however, you are more likely to lose privileges than gain them.

You lose the privilege to park closest to the building, even when it is raining or snowing, and begin to park as far out as possible so that the closest parking spaces are available for first-time visitors. You give up your seat in the sanctuary if needed so that a visitor can sit down. You give up the anonymity of being able to attend worship sporadically or as your schedule permits. You take on greater responsibility for serving both inside and outside the walls of the church. And, you make a commitment to share your financial resources to support the ministry and mission of the church.

As a church member you have entered into a covenant relationship, declaring, "I will support this church with my presence, service, giving, and prayers." Your membership signifies a commitment to grow deeper each day as you are transformed into Christlikeness, or made "*fully alive like Christ*" as we read in our scripture passage today.

Notice that our passage also speaks about our need to move "*rhythmically and easily with each other.*" This journey is not something we do alone. We do it in the context of Christian community. And, we do it in response to Christ.

How are you doing in fulfilling your membership expectations? Are you a contributing member of the body of Christ? Are you attending the worship service each week unless you are sick or out of town? Are you growing in your faith apart from worship? Are you actively serving God and sharing God with others? Are you giving in proportion to your income? Are you contributing to the peace and unity within the body? Are you praying daily for your church?

Take time to evaluate your commitment.

Reflection Questions

1. What privileges have you received by being a member of a club or organization? How is church membership different?

2. What are the specific membership expectations of your church?

3. How are you doing in fulfilling the basic expectations?

- Church
  1. Can you share the purpose and vision of your church?
  2. What are the distinctives of your church and denomination?
- Worship
  1. Are you in worship every week unless you are sick or out of town?
  2. Do you arrive early to prepare your heart for worship?
  3. Have you moved from being a spectator to being a participant?
- Growing Spiritually
  1. Have you obtained a good study Bible?
  2. Have you made Scripture reading and prayer a habit?
  3. Have you connected in a small group?
- Serving
  1. Have you discovered your spiritual gifts?
  2. Have you committed to regular service inside the walls of the church? Outside the walls of the church?
  3. Have you invited someone to church? Have you shared your faith story?
- Giving
  1. Have you done a personal budget to determine the financial gift you are able to commit to the mission and ministry of the church?
  2. Have you developed a plan to move toward tithing?
  3. Have you completed a commitment card?

Action Step

Evaluate your response from the reflection questions. Where do you have opportunity to grow? If you have not taken a next step since beginning this journey, consider what is holding you back. Do not wait for your church to guide you in this process. Initiate your next steps.

Church Membership:
Staying Committed

Scripture Reading: Hebrews 10:24-25

And let us consider how we may spur one another on toward love and good deeds, not giving up meeting together, as some are in the habit of doing, but encouraging one another—and all the more as you see the Day approaching.

Insight

Walking in my neighborhood is something I love and look forward to. My walks have often been a great time for prayer. I would pray for my neighbors as I passed their homes, I would pray for my children and family, I would pray for the church, I would pray for my husband and his job, and I would pray seeking God's guidance in my life. As I prayed, I would often find myself overwhelmed by the presence of God as I encountered him through nature. The singing of the birds, the smell of fall leaves or summer honeysuckle, and the light wind on my cheek gave me a sense of God's presence. I would marvel at God's power and majesty. Notice a key phrase in this confession—"*I would.*"

My habit has been to walk three or four times each week. Or at least, it used to be my habit. Something happened, I am not quite certain what or when, but my walks have now become sporadic. These days I may walk only one time a week. I have given up walking *as I had been in the habit of doing*. I really miss this activity in my life, but I have allowed other things to crowd it out.

This can happen in our spiritual lives as well. We make commitments that we have good intentions of keeping, but often give up our new habits without even realizing that we have done so. Other demands crowd into our schedules.

Today's Scripture passage was written to a group of people who were fairly new to the faith. The author encourages them not to become sporadic in their meeting together and tells them not to give up—a message that is still relevant today.

Developing good habits is a process that takes time and perseverance. Here are a few suggestions to help you keep your habit of being an active member of your church body:

1. Write down your goals and plans. Take small but attainable steps, increasing the likelihood of success.
2. Find accountability partners/friends. Share your plans, and ask that they hold you responsible.
3. Schedule time for worship, small group, and acts of service on your calendar, making these times a priority and safeguarding them so that other activities and commitments do not squeeze out this space.
4. Remember why your participation in the body of Christ is important.

Being a committed, active participant in the body of Christ must be a priority. It must be the new "normal" for the way you catch a new life.

Reflection Questions

1. List some of your habits. Are there any you want to break? Are there any you want to start?

2. Why is it easy to get out of the habit of regular worship and small group attendance?

3. How important is it that we have people hold us accountable? What does it mean to encourage one another?

Action Step

Identify someone to be your accountability partner. Schedule a time to meet. Share your plans. Invite your accountability partner to pray for you and to check on your progress. Is there someone for whom you should be an accountability partner?

Church Membership:
Praying for Your Church

Scripture Reading: John 17:1-26

After Jesus said this, he looked toward heaven and prayed:

"Father, the hour has come. Glorify your Son, that your Son may glorify you. For you granted him authority over all people that he might give eternal life to all those you have given him. Now this is eternal life: that they know you, the only true God, and Jesus Christ, whom you have sent. I have brought you glory on earth by finishing the work you gave me to do. And now, Father, glorify me in your presence with the glory I had with you before the world began.

"I have revealed you to those whom you gave me out of the world. They were yours; you gave them to me and they have obeyed your word. Now they know that everything you have given me comes from you. For I gave them the words you gave me and they accepted them. They knew with certainty that I came from you, and they believed that you sent me. I pray for them. I am not praying for the world, but for those you have given me, for they are yours. All I have is yours, and all you have is mine. And glory has come to me through them. I will remain in the world no longer, but they are still in the world, and I am coming to you. Holy Father, protect them by the power of your name, the name you gave me, so that they may be one as we are one. While I was with them, I protected them and kept them safe by that name you gave me. None has been lost except the one doomed to destruction so that Scripture would be fulfilled.

"I am coming to you now, but I say these things while I am still in the world, so that they may have the full measure of my joy within them. I have given them your word and the world has hated them, for they are not of the world

any more than I am of the world. My prayer is not that you take them out of the world but that you protect them from the evil one. They are not of the world, even as I am not of it. Sanctify them by the truth; your word is truth. As you sent me into the world, I have sent them into the world. For them I sanctify myself, that they too may be truly sanctified.

"My prayer is not for them alone. I pray also for those who will believe in me through their message, that all of them may be one, Father, just as you are in me and I am in you. May they also be in us so that the world may believe that you have sent me. I have given them the glory that you gave me, that they may be one as we are one—I in them and you in me—so that they may be brought to complete unity. Then the world will know that you sent me and have loved them even as you have loved me.

"Father, I want those you have given me to be with me where I am, and to see my glory, the glory you have given me because you loved me before the creation of the world.

"Righteous Father, though the world does not know you, I know you, and they know that you have sent me. I have made you known to them, and will continue to make you known in order that the love you have for me may be in them and that I myself may be in them."

Insight

Jesus has invited you to be a part of his redeeming work in the world. Though you may believe this invitation feels strange and unexpected, Jesus has chosen us to be his visible presence here on earth. As members of the body of Christ, we are the hands and feet of Christ called to carry out his work. One way to take part in this work is to offer your prayers.

In John 17, we read one of Jesus' prayers. First, Jesus prays for himself (vv. 1-5), asking his Father to glorify him in order that he might glorify God. Second, Jesus prays for his disciples (vv. 6-19), asking for their harmony. He prays that they would know full joy, that they would be protected as they go into the world to do God's work, and that they would be holy. Finally, Jesus prays for the future members of the body of Christ (vv. 20-23), asking for them to be one in unity. He prays that they would know the love of Christ and demonstrate that love to others.

Take time to pray for yourself, your church, your church leaders, and those in your community who have yet to say, "I do," to Christ. Use the example of Jesus' prayer in John 17 as a model for your own.

Pray first for yourself:
- That God will be glorified because of your completing the work he has given to you to do
- That you will remain faithful and be open to the leading of the Holy Spirit and the work of Christ in your life

Pray for your church leaders and fellow church members:
- That your church's vision is God's vision
- For harmony among your church leaders and members
- For perseverance and protection as you share the love of Christ in the world
- That in everything, your church leaders and members will know immeasurable joy
- That each of your members will know the full depth of the love of Christ and demonstrate this love to others

Pray for those who are not yet members of the body of Christ:
- That they will be open to the invitation
- For unity with other churches in your community

Your prayers are one of the ways you partner in the important work of your church. As we approach the end of our study together, here is my prayer for you: *"Be assured that from the first day we heard of you, we haven't stopped praying for you, asking God to give you wise minds and spirits attuned to his will, and so acquire a thorough understanding of the ways in which God works. We pray that you'll live well for the Master, making him proud of you as you work hard in his orchard. As you learn more and more how God works, you will learn how to do your work. We pray that you'll have the strength to stick it out over the long haul—not the grim strength of gritting your teeth but the glory-strength God gives. It is strength that endures the unendurable and spills over into joy, thanking the Father who makes us strong enough to take part in everything bright and beautiful that he has for us"* (Colossians 1:9-12, THE MESSAGE).

Reflection Questions

1. How do you see prayer as an important way you participate in God's redeeming work in the world?

2. What bullet points would you add to the prayer for yourself? Your church leaders and members? Future church members?

3. What does it mean to be in "unity" with one another? How are you helping to unify the church?

Action Step

Take time to write a note of encouragement to one of the leaders in your church. Express thanksgiving and appreciation for his or her ministry. Let this person know you have been praying for him or her both personally and as a leader in the church.

Day 40

Church Membership:
Catch a New Life

Scripture Reading: 1 John 2:28

And now, children, stay with Christ. Live deeply in Christ. Then we'll be ready for him when he appears, ready to receive him with open arms. (THE MESSAGE)

Insight

The score of the semifinal game in the Kansas State 6A High School playoffs was 17 to 14. The trailing Falcons had the ball on their opponent's 26 yard line as the clock ticked away the final minutes of the game. It was fourth and ten. If the Falcons failed to move the ball 10 yards, the season would be over. The play was called, "62-Go!" The crowd stood on its feet in anticipation. The quarterback looked right then left, and he released the ball. As the ball sailed into the air, all eyes in both stands followed to see where it would go. Then the unexpected happened—the ball had been thrown to the wide receiver, who was running toward the end zone fighting off double coverage. The receiver looked back over his left shoulder, lunged forward fully extending his body, and with outstretched arms caught the ball for the game-winning touchdown!

The newspaper editorial in the sports section the next day called it the "Catch of the Year," and to this day, we still refer to it as the "catch of a lifetime." The wide receiver was my son, and I know firsthand the complete exhilaration and joy he felt making that catch. It is something he will remember for a lifetime.

There are several notable factors to consider in this scenario:

1. The quarterback and receiver were a part of a larger team in which each member had an important job to do in order to make the play possible.
2. The quarterback threw the ball expecting it to be caught. He had confidence in his wide receiver. They had developed a plan for this play, and now was the time to execute it.
3. The wide receiver was in position, ready to receive the ball with outstretched hands.

For the past forty days, you have been considering what it means to catch a new life as you take steps toward becoming an active member in the life of your church. You have discovered you have an important job to do and God has invited you to be a part of his work in the world.

Throughout this journey, you have created action steps. Now is the invitation to fully execute your plans! If catching a football can bring that much joy, imagine the joy God has in store for you as you catch a new life. All God requires is that you be in position, ready to receive with outstretched hands and open arms.

Discovering the call God has on your life is the true catch of a lifetime.

Reflection Questions
1. What does it mean to have outstretched arms, ready to receive Christ?

2. Name the areas where you feel you have grown the most over these past forty days.

3. What has challenged you the most?

Action Step

Stay committed to the journey of becoming an active member. Refer back to your journal and notes as a guide. Pray without ceasing.

Journal Pages

Journal Pages

Journal Pages

Journal Pages

Journal Pages

Journal Pages

Journal Pages